A Pocket Book of Grace

Copyright ©2019 Mosope Macarthy-Chiadika
pocketbookofgrace@gmail.com. Supported by Sixthway Company. All rights reserved. First paperback edition printed 2019 in the
United Kingdom. A catalogue record for this book is available from the British Library.
ISBN 978-1-913455-01-9
No part of this book shall be reproduced or transmitted in any form or by any means, electronic or mechanical, including photocopying, recording, or by any information retrieval system without prior written permission of the publisher. Published by Scribblecity Publications.
Printed in Great Britain.
Although every precaution has been taken in the preparation of this book, the publisher and author assume no responsibility for errors or omissions. Neither is any liability assumed for damages resulting from the use of this information contained herein.
Scripture quotations marked NLT are taken from the Holy Bible, New Living Translation, copyright © 1996, 2004, 2015 by Tyndale House Foundation. Used by permission of Tyndale House Publishers, Inc., Carol Stream, Illinois 60188. All rights reserved.

Acknowledgements

I am unreservedly grateful to Almighty God my Saviour, who inspired this work and provided every resource to accomplish it. To Him be all the glory.

It's usually said that "it takes a village" to raise a child. In like terms, I would say it took a community to make *A Pocket Book of Grace* a reality. When I received the inspiration in May 2015 to write the book, I embarked on the journey and tagged it the *Labour of Love Project* (LoLP). From start to finish, everyone involved contributed a measure of their labour of love to create this landmark biography.

Special thanks to my mother, Grace Olayide Macarthy who is the subject of the book. Your strength and courage to share the story of your life stems largely from your walk of living faith and trust as you said in "the Redeemer of my soul." Your story embodies the grace of our Lord Jesus Christ, the love of the heavenly Father and the presence of the Holy Spirit in diverse ways and forms in your life. Just like Caleb in the Bible you have obtained the inheritance of God's faithfulness to fulfil His good Word. Thank you for your labour of love in sharing your story for His glory!

I'd especially like to thank the LoLP team - Pam Verhagen, Judy Yearwood and Miriam Mweneake. Your insights, skills, time and most of all, your willing and open hearts to this project is invaluable. Special thanks to Pam (Mama P) for the meticulous typing of interview sessions. I continue to savour the experiences we shared.

Thank you to everyone who took out time to express their heartfelt testimonials in their different relationships with Grace (to make it more personal). Your responses revealed an amazing inspiration, and the impact of God's love and grace in and through her life. Your labour of love is much appreciated.

Sincere thanks to Mrs Yewande Akinyemi for sharing some memories and insight as the eldest sister in the entire Macarthy family. Thank you Sister for your prayer and encouragement.

I would like to thank Pastor Colin & Mrs Dorselie Gittens for their spiritual support over the years. Thank you for your constant labour of love.

My appreciation to everyone who gave their support in different ways to make this biography a reality.

Thank you to Barbara and her team at Scribblecity Publications, for your skills and technical abilities to put the work together.

Finally, I must express my gratitude to my

readers for accepting my invitation to journey with me through this inspiring story of God's grace.

Mama Grace Olayide Macarthy

Dedication

This book is thankfully dedicated to the Lord Jesus Christ, the Redeemer.

Also in loving memory of Oluwarotimi Babatunde Macarthy.

Contents

Foreword	xi
Introduction	1
Character	5
Royalty	10
Endowment	14
Compassion	18
Romance	21
Redemption	26
Goodness	34
Righteousness	40
Gratitude	44
Confidence	50
Conviction	52
Encouragement	58
Covenant	64
Ambassador	82
Counsel	87
Afterword	110
Reward	131
Expressions	154
Endnotes	157

Foreword

A biography is a thoughtful and honouring work of love. Quite different from an autobiography, it is an impactful way of taking inventory of a human life in its course. It is like giving flowers to the living. It speaks volumes of the many deposits that individual has made, and continues to make, into the lives of many.

The pages that follow attest to this truth in reference to the God-ordained life of Grace Olayide Macarthy. *A Pocket Book of Grace* chronicles the steadfast, gracious, consistent life and testimony of this woman of God. It succinctly captures her life's purpose, and in doing so challenges its readers to emulate her Godly qualities.

Grace is indeed among the meagre 6% of Christians today, in North America, who are still willing to share their faith with others and lead individuals to seek salvation in Christ. Her name is not a coincidence of choice, but rather an intentional God-incidence to live out the reality of its meaning. Ephesians 2: 6 reminds us of this truth: "For it is by grace we have been saved, through faith and this is not from yourself, it is the gift of God not by works, so that no one can boast." It could accurately be said that Grace lives out this verse as if it were her mission statement.

She is careful and quick to remind you that the works she has accomplished, in Jesus' name, are credited to Him and Him alone. She understands, both from experience and a close walk with God, what it means to listen and be sensitive to the still small voice of God. This is very refreshing.

The writer to the Hebrews challenges us to consider how we may spur one another on towards love and good deeds (10:24). This is exactly how you will feel when you read the captivating stories/experiences Grace has been permitted to have, thus far in life. She has, and continues to stimulate good works to all those who have known and observed her walk of faith in Christ. If you have had the privilege of being in her presence, and have had her pray or speak into your life, then you know what I mean. If you haven't, seek for an opportunity to spend a few moments with this saint. I speak from experience. My wife Dorselie and I, have been recipients of her prayer ministry, and have been refreshed by her Godly counsel. She is truly a vessel that has been set apart to bring glory and honour to the name of Jesus. And she's a breath of fresh air.

The stories that are told in this little volume, attest to a life that is sold out to God. The outcome of the tests and vicissitudes of life she has faced, has fueled her boldness to represent Christ well. Consequently, she has become a threat to the enemy. She looks for and relishes every opportunity to share her faith with others.

God's unmerited favour, that epitomizes her name, exudes from her as she tells her God stories.

As you read this biography, my prayer for you is this: that you will catch a fresh glimpse of what it means to "love the Lord your God with all your heart and with all your soul and with all your strength." (Deut. 6:5). It is for this purpose He created us. I also pray that these stories will ultimately spur you on to love your neighbour as yourself. In this way you too will make a significant impact for God. And if perchance you have not yet surrendered your life to Christ, my prayer is that you will allow the conviction of the Holy Spirit to have His way.

It is, therefore, with prayer and these thoughts in mind that I commend *A Pocket Book of Grace* to you.

Colin A. Gittens
Pastor

"Now that I am old and gray, do not abandon me O God. Let me proclaim your power to this new generation, your mighty miracles to all who come after me." Psalm 71:18 (NLT)

"For we have heard of your faith in Christ Jesus and your love for all God's people, which come from your confident hope of what God has reserved for you in heaven. You have had this expectation ever since you first heard the truth of the Good News. This same Good News that came to you is going out all over the world. It is bearing fruit everywhere by changing lives, just as it changed your lives from the day you first heard and understood the truth about God's wonderful grace." Colossians 1: 4-6 (NLT)

"No matter what her other virtues – a generous nature, a gift for hospitality, beauty, intelligence, culinary expertise, an excellent wife to her husband or mother to her children, a community leader – nothing makes a woman more extraordinary than her faith. This was true in Bible times, and it still applies today." Excerpt from: *The Extraordinary Mother (2007)* by John Macarthur, Author and President of "Grace to You" radio program.

Introduction

The Old and New Testaments are filled with stories of men and women, old and young, from diverse cultural and economic backgrounds. A very distinct attribute that can be gleaned from many of these characters is the grace of God they all experienced. With their strengths and weaknesses, faults and virtues, the grace of God came through in all of their stories. They were ordinary people who lived extraordinary lives as they learned to trust and walk by faith with God's involvement in their lives. They found grace in His sight and their stories became reference points for others during the times they lived in, and to the present day. Today, God continues to pour out His grace enabling us to find love, truth, hope, faith, forgiveness, courage, purpose, strength, and wisdom for life's journey. The grace of God can be described as His love-provoked favour. It seeks out a person without any effort or qualification. It is unmerited, unearned and undeserved. God initiates grace to reveal His unconditional love according to His plan and purpose. In similar ways the stories of these individuals who fill the pages of the Bible are our stories as we too need the grace of God in our lives.

The New Testament reveals Jesus as God's grace personified. His call reaches to the entire world, and as many who believe and receive Him are given the right to become the children of God (John 1:12 paraphrased). The 1828 Webster's Dictionary states that "Grace is the power of God poured into us free of charge to enable us do with ease what we could not do on our own with any amount of effort or struggle."[1] Dr. Jeffery Rus, a profound teacher of God's Word defines Grace as "the empowerment of the presence of God, enabling you to be all that you are called to be, and to do all that you are called to do."

My mother is the main subject of this biographical work that I am humbled to write, and she is one among so many who have received the miracle of God's grace and love through Christ. In the years I have known her, I could describe her as a woman who wears many hats. She is a daughter, sibling, wife, mother, friend, neighbour, business woman, employer, minister of God, mother-in-law, grandmother, great grandmother, and mentor. Through these relationships, valuable lessons of life have been learned. One thing which stands out in particular is how God reveals His grace to a heart yielded to Him: "Grace is understood best within the context of relationship. After all, it is only within the mystery and complexity of relationships that grace is experienced, but not just any grace, the grace of God."[2]

My mother certainly isn't perfect but serves a perfect God. Her upward relationship with Him is the flow through which her downward relationships are directed. As the author, I write this story in a personally inspired thought of GRACE; as *God's Riches At Christ's Expression*. Suffice to say, it is no coincidence that my subject's name is "Grace" can we say God's plan? In this light, I invite you to embark on a journey with me as we discover, learn, and glean from her story, the riches of God's grace that inspired the writing of this book. My hope is that you will be inspired and encouraged in your life's journey because the story of God's grace is your story too.

Mosope Macarthy-Chiadika
2019

Character

We drove through the deserted streets of Ontario. It was Friday July 1st 2016, Fête du Canada, otherwise known as Canada Day celebration. We were on our way to my sister's house. As we arrived, she welcomed us and ushered us into the living room where my mother awaited our arrival.

Grace Olayide Macarthy was born on Wednesday the 19th of March, 1930 to Emmanuel Jaiyesimi Ogundimu and Celina Olamide Ogundimu. Pam curiously enquired from Grace if she knew the day of the week she was born. Brows knitted together, she thought for a few minutes,

"I'm not so sure about that," she replied with a shake of her head.

Of course she did not know, but immediately David, my son, who came with us swiftly pulled out his phone and with a few clicks exclaimed, "Wednesday!"

At birth she was named *Olayide Alagbala*, in the language of the Yoruba tribe of south-western Nigeria. It denotes the arrival of honor and wealth, a person who has vast lands and possessions. You could hear a pin drop, as we all sat spellbound listening attentively as she took us back to her early years. Her voice rich with age, yet very strong floated across the room. She spoke about one distinctive thing from her early days, the dark birthmark that peered from behind her left ear. Gently moving her body, she turned her head to reveal the patch sitting on the base of her ear.

Her middle name, Grace, which is her preferred name, was given on the occasion of her Christian baptism. She recalled the event.

"I was not with my parents and siblings when my parents planned a family baptism for all the children. I lived with a family who were close friends, and who needed some help with housekeeping at that time. My siblings had the opportunity of choosing a Christian name for themselves but since I was not at home to choose mine, my parents with my siblings' support decided to choose one for me. They chose the name "Grace", and it became my middle name from baptism."

We listened with much interest as she continued, "As I grew up, it had a greater connection with me, even though I didn't understand its meaning then."

It was a large family with six siblings: four sisters and two brothers. The first child of her parents was Mrs Elizabeth Ayoola Oshodi lovingly called "Mama Kekere", meaning "little mother", by her siblings and extended family. Two brothers came after her: Mr Phillip Adekanbi Ogundimu and Mr Solomon Oladipupo Ogundimu. Her sister, Mrs Christiana Olagunju Akitoye was born after them, and then, along came another sister, Mrs Esther Adewunmi Bada. Grace was next, and finally there was yet another sister, Mrs Janet Olayemi Karonwi.

Those early years were spent at Ebute-Meta in the Mainland of Lagos State where she was born. It is a large, well governed urban area known for its commercial and residential vibrancy. Grace's father ruled as king of one of its regions known as Oto. He ascended the much-coveted Oto throne at the age of seventy-two and reigned as the Oloto of Oto (Osuro II) for eighteen years before his passing.

Palace life for the Ogundimus was both an exciting and challenging experience. They were in constant public view, as a family, but still had to maintain a stable family life of love and support. The palace had a boisterous atmosphere with traditional activities within, outside, and in the larger state. It was a rallying point for the highs and lows of the region. My mother has many good memories of those years as a princess. Family members were always around, and they enjoyed the hustle and bustle of palace life, lived happily, cooking and eating together, as well as planning community events especially the festival celebrations which drew crowds from near and far. Another distinct feature of palace life was gifts brought by various people to the palace for her father, "Baba Oloye" (meaning "the ruling father" as he was fondly called), and his household. He would often mediate between the people and resolve conflicts in the community. As a result, it was customary to bring gifts to him, an act which depicted acceptance of and respect for his reign. The gifts included items such as fish, live animals like goats and sheep, crafts, drinks, wine and spirits and more.

Grace's mother fondly called "Mama Agba", meaning "older mother" by her children and wider family, reigned as the *Olori* - the royal Queen of Oto palace. She was from the

Johnson family of Badagry, a coastal town on the outskirts of Lagos State. A town of significance, Badagry was the place where slave trade began in Nigeria.

Its sea port was the route through which slaves were transported out of the shores of Nigeria to overseas countries. Coincidentally, it also became the town where Christian missionaries from the west first came and settled many years after the abolishment of slave trade.

Royalty

Grace's memories of her parents date back to her early childhood. She recalls that her mother was the stricter of the two. Mama Agba was a great influence in encouraging her children in the Christian faith, and she always insisted on regular attendance at church. Grace reminisces how her mother would not put up with any nonsense from her children especially if they didn t want to go to church. She chuckled as she remembered, "we wouldn't eat if we didn't go!" At this, everyone in the room burst out laughing. Her sturdy frame shook with laughter. She quickly stated it was a blessing to have had such a godly mother.

As for her father, Grace described him as being very cool headed yet assertive. She remembered how he would sometimes discuss the Bible with the neighbours.

Grace saw her mother as the rallying point of the family. She described the matriarch as a pillar of love and affection to all around her. Both parents had a high standard of upbringing for their children, with the Christian faith being the bedrock of their values. As parents, their children's education was an important aspect of their lives. Grace was well behaved and often pointed to as an example of good behaviour. The children all enjoyed the love, care and nurture of their parents, and this foundation ensured their future success. Her parents were not rich, yet they did everything possible to make sure the basic needs of their children were met, and made enormous personal financial sacrifices towards their education and general wellbeing.

In later years, despite the challenges that came with having another wife as was the custom in those days when her father became king of the region, Grace revealed that her parents maintained a good marriage all through their life time. Her mother lived with her father in the palace throughout his life. Years after his passing at ninety years old, she continued to live in the palace till her passing.

From her growing up years, Grace's favourite foods have always been rice, amala and garri. The last two are made from dried yam and cassava tubers respectively. They are ground into flour, cooked into a solid paste by stirring in boiling water, and then enjoyed with either leafy vegetables, okra or melon soups, meat and fish. Grace savours her favourite foods even in her old age.

Grace enjoyed the luxury of a lake on the Mainland where she grew up. She expressed her creativity with jewellery and crafts made from seashells. She would first design and paint on canvas before transferring onto fabric. This creative ability served her well later in her successful fashion business. Grace and her best friend, Kubura Balogun, a Muslim, would go to the lake together with other friends to play and have fun especially during the hot summer months. Grace was athletic, often racing on the hot sands of the shore of the lake. She also enjoyed playing cards and *Ayo*, a local board game played with pebbles.

Holidays, especially Christmas and the New Year were special. The celebrations were marked with beautiful outfits, scrumptious food, and visiting friends. These were always a time of getting together for the family. "We would share the experiences of the year and pray for God's covering for another year."

Fondly remembering the gifts she received while growing up, one in particular, was her favourite, a picture frame from all her siblings that read "we all love you, you are the best."

Engraved on the frame was the royal seal, the symbol of her father's crown. The gift was signed by all her siblings. It was precious to her; unfortunately, it was mislaid as she moved from place to place.

Her interests were always piqued by world events, as she loved to follow trends, and be up to date with things going on around her. She vaguely remembered a caption she saw in "Pilot", a local newspaper, which read "show the light and the people will find the way." This phrase became etched in her mind and guided her endeavours and relationships in life. Arguably this caption perhaps was a self-fulfilling prophecy that later connected her to a personal relationship with the true Light. (John 1:9)

As a child, her parents gave her a small allowance (shillings and pence then) which she used to meet her personal needs. The responsibilities of house chores were shared with her siblings. She was quite caring and would often help those who had challenges. Her words and actions always brought great encouragement.

Endowment

For her elementary education, Grace attended Patience Modern School for six years where she enjoyed being part of the athletics team. "I loved to run!" she exclaimed. Her secondary school years were more engaging where she spent five years at the Salvation Army Secondary School and graduated with the national school leaving certificate. Her favourite subject was mathematics, while history and geography were the two subjects she liked least. With her flair for creativity, she appreciated subjects that enhanced her designs. This paid off, as her interest in Math helped tremendously with calculating measurements later in her fashion career.

After her secondary school in 1945, she proceeded to learn fashion and sewing at the Macaulay Sewing Institute at Broad Street on Lagos Island where she obtained a Fashion Design certificate. On completion in 1948, she took private jobs that helped enhance her skills as well as earn some money. A few years later, she was engaged and married. Years into married life, she set up her own business called *Go Smart and Sons Fashion House* which she ran for over twenty years. In 1958, her husband needed to take a professional course, so they both travelled together to England for a year. Grace made the most of the opportunity while there. She improved her knowledge by taking a course on how to make belts, buttons and buckles with different machines. On their return from England, with her husband's support, Grace ordered some machines from overseas for her business. She also sold fabrics, lace materials, shoes, purses and jewellery ordered from overseas. With over ten staff working with her, her business grew and became well established. During busy seasons of the year like Christmas, her staff slept on the premises in order to keep up with demands and deadlines for orders!

Grace had contracts with some community schools to sew uniforms. We listened attentively to her fashion exploits. Her sense of duty and diligence was clearly portrayed in her desire for excellence. As a daughter, this brought back lovely memories to me. I reminisced on how my mother designed and made clothes for her clients back then. Her children and husband topped her list, as we always showcased her designs. Whenever we attended church or birthday parties dressed in exquisite new outfits, people would always enquire about who made the clothes. Mother's sense of industry and resourcefulness had a positive impact on her family and others who knew her over the years. It is one of the legacies we benefited from. Feeling humble and thankful, Grace added, "I didn't know Christ personally in all those years, but God gave me those ideas. I would come up with a design and always everyone would rush for it." The designs were indeed exceptional, carrying a 'divine touch' which made her clients choose to 'Go Smart!'

Looking back, God also had a higher purpose in all this. As the master designer, He was working behind the scene in her life, weaving her story to reveal His ever-unfailing love and grace in a very personal way. Grace mentioned the challenges she faced when she finally committed her life to Jesus. In a few words she explained, "All forces come against you when you are open about your faith. God was faithful and never failed me. He enabled me to become an overcomer."

Grace eventually gave up her business and decided to give her time fully to serving the Lord. She interjected with the story of the rich young ruler [3] who Jesus told to sell all he had and give to the poor, but he couldn't, and he went away sorrowing. For Grace it was a difficult decision, but she said, "Nothing is too hard, for His way is different from my way and I could understand." She broke into a song, "When He calls, I will answer, I will follow and work for my Lord." At our request, we paused to take a photo of her bible. The black leather cover was frayed; worn-out from constant use over the years. The pages quite delicate, revealing the faded coloured markings that underlined the different verses. If it could speak, it would probably tell of wars that were won by holding on to its contents. We took a short break to have a quick drink and some snacks while Judy, one of our team members had to leave for another engagement.

Compassion

We resumed the session with Grace revealing how the interview had brought back so many memories, although there were many events she could no longer remember clearly. Unforgettable was the positive impact left by her parents, siblings, and others. Grace described her mother, Celina as "sunshine" in her life. She spoke of her as the greatest human influence she ever had. She watched her mother demonstrate a life of caring and giving to others within her resources. This legacy was passed down, as I have also seen my mother demonstrate this quality over the years.

We sensed a little emotion in her voice as Grace described the events that preceded the passing of her mother. The day before, her mother had called her on the phone and prayed for her, affirming God's protection over her and her family. The next day, to her shock, she received a phone call from the palace with the news of Mama Agba's passing. It was a peaceful transition to eternity. Grace's niece, Bisi Ogundimu, fondly called "Bisi Oto" (because she lived in the palace) gave details of the event. She narrated how she was attending a party at another wing of the palace that night. Mama Agba not wanting the young girl stranded outside through the night, sent a message to her to be back before she locked the door. Not long after, Bisi came back from the party, and prepared for bed. In the early hours of the morning, she heard Mama Agba exclaim "Jesu!" ("Jesus" in the Yoruba language) three times. Her thought was that she was starting her usual morning prayer. It was a dramatic experience for Bisi, because as she drifted back to sleep, she recalled that she saw what looked like two angelic figures in the room carry Mama Agba away. She woke up suddenly, startled by what she had seen, and called out to her in her usual way, "Mama Agba! Mama Agba!" When there was no reply, Bisi ran out of the room, quite frightened. She called the attention of the palace residents, who came and confirmed that Mama Agba had passed away. She was ninety years of age. My grandmother was a beacon of light within the demands of tradition that came with her role as an *Olori*.[4] She made no compromise of her Christian faith and lived it out in her personal, family and community life. "My mother journeyed in the path of the Gospel of Christ," Grace added. And this same faith of my grandmother was transmitted to her generation and is reflected in and through my mother's life.

Romance

A lovely cool mid-week morning, our team was back to interview Grace. We expected heat and humidity, but the sun hadn't risen fully. The roads were clear with little traffic as we drove smoothly. Pam and I planned a short session for the day while my younger daughter, Newness, came along to help with the recording. It was a perfect way for her to share a summer morning with grandma.

The room reverberated with bursts of laughter as Grace let us into her love life. Robert Oladapo Macarthy, won her heart in a romantic relationship that started between them when she lived with her eldest sister, Mama Kekere, at Bankole Street, in downtown Lagos Island popularly called "Isale-Eko." "There were other young suitors, but they were not God's choice for me, Grace said."

He was from the same neighborhood, and usually walked past her sister's house. Grace caught Robert's attention during his many walks back from work because not long after, he became a regular visitor in their home.

Big sister did not encourage male visitors to call without a chaperone. However, Robert would still drop in when he left the office to spend time with his girlfriend. They were not allowed out alone, and he had to be content with house visits only! Grace's sister was very firm about that in the early days. As time went by, they became closer and their love grew. Grace described him as "very quiet, gentle and loving."

"He was a sociable and handsome man as you can see from his children," she added, indicating in my direction with a big smile.

My parents got married on Thursday, April 17, 1952. At the time, Robert was an active, though nominal Christian, who loved to be involved with church activities and was a member of the choir and the Youth club. He played soccer and loved to watch wrestling matches. His interest in wrestling encouraged him years later to serve as a member of the Board of the Nigerian Wrestling Association on a national level. This position gave him the opportunity to lead the Nigerian team and delegation to an international wrestling competition in Canada in the late seventies.

As she spoke about her husband, her eyes

lit up and her face radiated with love. Her voice bubbled with teen excitement and her enthusiasm was contagious. Robert joined the Boys' Brigade of Nigeria for the mainland region and rose to the position of Captain during his lifetime. He started his career in government service as a young postal clerk with the Federal Ministry of Post and Telecommunications. With diligence and hard work, he rose with promotions to become the Director of Personnel (Human Resources). He worked for thirty-three years before his retirement in 1975. After his retirement from service, he worked as the Human Resource and Administrative head for an automobile company, and later with a manufacturing company. Grace recounted that her married life was quite good. Like every other couple, they had their challenges, but learned to settle issues and move on.

Daily life was a pleasant experience as the children grew up. At the end of each day, they made it a point of duty to come home and spend time together as a family. She listed the names of their children: Her first child was Oluwarotimi Macarthy; then there were her eldest daughters, Oloruntoyin Ogunsan and Oluwayemisi Abrahams. Next were the twins,

Kehinde (Kenny) Macarthy; and Taiwo Olusola Macarthy; and finally, Mosopelowooluwa Chiadika; Oluwapelumi Macarthy; and Modupe Mann.

As a mother, raising her children was a joy but not without challenges. She attested to God's grace in helping her bring up her children in the way of the Lord as the Bible encourages in Proverbs 22:6. Though as parents, Grace and Robert played different roles in the upbringing of their children, Grace mentioned how Robert took his position as a husband and father "very seriously." He dearly loved his wife and children. He aimed high for them and encouraged them especially in their education and was always ready to give advice when needed.

As the family grew, Robert and Grace decided to move from their rented apartment at 36 Odunfa Street, Ebute-Meta on the Mainland of Lagos State. Their first ever big purchase together was some plots of land where they gradually built a two-storey residence located at 39 Falolu Street, Surulere, a more conservative area of the mainland. This was where the children all grew up and had their secondary and post-secondary education. It was also here that Grace's sewing and fashion business was established. She had the entire front of the ground floor as her work and showroom, as well as another area that accommodated fabrics and other sewing equipment. While her husband was at work, and the children at school, she would spend her time developing her business.

In those years, she described herself and her husband as nominal Christians. They went to church mainly on Sundays and on special occasions, to fulfil religious obligations. They and their children attended St. Jude's Anglican Church, her husband's local church where he attended.

Redemption

Grace shared extensively the major challenges she and Robert faced as parents including Taiwo's developmental disability, and the medical diagnosis of sickle cell disease in three of the children. She would often watch helplessly as they went through episodes of painful and distressing crises. These experiences were always laced with recurring bouts of fear, uncertainty, and frequent hospital admissions. It took a toll on all emotionally, financially and even spiritually. In December 1973, the family went through a dark period when the first child and son was lost to this disease at the age of twenty-one. It was devastating, a time of deep grief and pain. All hope seemed lost. Yet, in the midst of the deep sorrow, God was working His plan, to take centre stage in the life of this family. He desired to reveal His will as the Author of life and salvation. He desired to dethrone the kingdom of darkness and enthrone His Kingdom of light through the authority of

Christ in the family.[5]

Grace recalled how one of her husband's staff members at the office who was a believer in Christ visited the family at that time. He came with an invitation to a revival crusade through the ministry of Reverend Agemiro from Brazil. He encouraged them to take Taiwo to the crusade for prayers.

The entire family attended the crusade in January 1974, a month after the intensely difficult loss. Grace revealed that it was at this crusade that the family gave their lives to Jesus in a real and personal way when an altar call was made by the minister. After the crusade, Grace made a personal decision to start attending the Free Gospel Centre, Mushin, which is now known as Winners Gospel Centre. This local church had hosted the crusade. Gradually, Grace grew in her new relationship with Jesus and she would often take the children with her to church. Confidently Grace proclaimed, "When light comes, darkness goes! It is not about religion or walking in our ego. It is about commitment to God through faith in Christ." When asked what changes took place in her home after her commitment to Jesus, Grace responded that the challenges didn't stop there. "I learned to trust Him as a new born baby and continued on a beautiful journey with Him. A child is not yet ready to walk the day he or she is born, but they learn gradually. So it is with spiritual babies in the Kingdom of God. You begin the journey with Him and He opens your eyes gradually. No matter how poor, rich or beautiful you are, you learn that He is in control."

Her thirst for the Lord grew, and after a year of regularly attending church services, she gradually became involved in different church teams resulting in evident changes in her life and home. She described this growth as "God's mercy, power and intervention where Jesus is Lord." Consequently, her husband joined her. Though he continued to attend St. Jude's church, from time to time, he would go with his wife to her church, especially during special services. "Light had now come. The truth transformed him, and his friends at his old church saw a difference in him; many eventually gave their lives to Jesus because of the change they witnessed." Grace revealed, "This transformation continued, and God's grace allowed us to live totally for His name without looking back. We had many challenges, but God's grace helped us overcome." Grace unreservedly spoke of this grace of God in her life and family with a deep trust in the God that took her brokenness and despair, mended every piece and filled her emptiness with His love and grace. Jesus came into her life and family as the game changer and re-wrote their history. She had so much to attest to the faithfulness of God in her life and family through the years.

She recalled an incident when God miraculously intervened in the life of her son, Kenny, who now lives in England. He was in school outside Lagos and fell very ill with a sickle-cell crisis. He was taken to hospital, unknown to the family in Lagos. Grace revealed how God opened her eyes in a vision like He did for Elijah[6] and she saw a casket being prepared. God assured her that He was in control and she should not be afraid as He was going to intervene. He gave her such peace that she knew the plan of the enemy would not succeed. With His peace in her heart, she travelled to Abeokuta, in Ogun state, about a hundred kilometres from Lagos where Kehinde was in school. She was directed to the hospital, and when she got there, things were not looking very good for him, but she believed the Lord would fulfil His promise to intervene. She stayed there with him for weeks until he gradually began to mend and was eventually discharged. Today, she continues to thank God for His grace in this situation.

Grace recalled yet another episode of God's intervention. Her daughter, Taiwo, was sweeping the room and unknowingly threw an envelope that contained a large sum of money into the garbage bin. She was registered as a contractor with the Lagos State government, a business she took up later to help the family financially. She received a contract for road repairs, and the money was meant to pay the construction site workers. Grace searched everywhere for the missing envelope. She eventually told her husband, and together, they searched diligently. He told her not to worry. They would go to the bank and use the title deed of their house to cover the contract. Yet she continued to search for six more days. The next day she heard the garbage truck coming up the street and it was raining. Suddenly an inner voice prompted her to check the main garbage bin outside the house, "otherwise the garbage men will take the money away." At this point, the truck was only two houses away, another frantic search revealed a damp envelope with the money right at the bottom. What a relief! What joy!

Grace concluded this interview session with a reminder that love was the key ingredient in bringing up the children. It was important to express unconditional love to their children. "You trust God to be in charge. He is the only one who can orchestrate their lives. We are His instruments, and He is the one who can complete the job in their lives. It is not up to the mother." She gave an example from the Bible about the unrelenting widow and the judge and encouraged us to be consistent and persistent in prayer saying, "Jesus Himself is our supreme example, only then will God's peace flood our hearts." And even when troubles come, Grace remarked that, "the Lord is more than sufficient to bear the burden for us and will continue to the end." Speaking about challenges in the family, especially with sickle cell, Grace also pointed to her daughter, Sope, as an example of God's handiwork: "To see her is to see Christ living in her. Praise be to Him! It is Christ alone.

It is God's message of power and intervention in the midst of the impossible. Jesus is Lord," she spoke with conviction.

Grace is proud of her children and grandchildren, and thankful to God as she sees them walking in His light with endurance. She continues to pray, hope and dream for her posterity that the Lord will continue to orchestrate their lives and they will not relent. Grace remarked that being a mother is a continuous job. A mother looks to heaven and help comes from the Lord.
It's really not all up to her. It is God who can complete the job in their lives. "I am not a good or bad mother, but one saved by the power of the Almighty God," Grace added.

Her dear husband passed away on May 15, 2003, after they celebrated over fifty years of marriage. Sensing a prompting of the Holy Spirit in the conversation, she interjected, "The love we had for each other made us forget that there is death. But thank God that we are not dead!" Since his passing, Grace admitted that God's peace has continued to rule in the family because He is the one that has all things in His hands.

It was an interview session of mixed emotions

as Grace expressed the trials and triumphs that laced her family life. Her life-changing encounter with God through faith in Jesus, brought transformation not only to her life, but eventually to her husband and children. Her faith and tenacity in the Lord has continued to be a source of inspiration for many who have also come to experience the work of God's grace in their lives.

Goodness

Two days later, Pam and I were back at my sister's house to continue where we left off. Pam asked that I say an opening prayer for the session. I prayed for wisdom, anointing, peace and that God would make this process impactful and a blessing to people.

As usual Mom was smartly dressed and ready for the day's session. She expressed her appreciation for God's grace on everyone with the work at hand.

"I didn't plan or expect to have my biography written, she began. When I spoke to the Lord about it, He told me it was in His plan, and that He is in perfect control. That gave me peace, and the joy I have to do this," she said.

We had much to ask and Grace had a lot to talk about regarding her faith journey with the Lord over many decades. She recalled experiences that revealed His grace, mercy, provision and faithfulness to her. "As I said, we gave our lives at a crusade. Before then, we were regular church goers and like others we worked from our own ego. We did everything in our own sufficiency not knowing we were empty. We didn't know that Jesus was the Owner of heaven and earth. We didn't know Him personally or how we offended Him with our sin. But when the time was right, He beckoned us to Himself. Since then, He has not left me alone. He directs my steps and commands me to read only His Word."

Grace affirmed how the Lord told her He would be showing Himself to her through His Word, and truly He did, for which she is so thankful. "He has continued till today," she added happily. Asked what life was like after she gave her life to Jesus, and the change that came with the spiritual awakening, Grace responded, "He continued to work in my heart and train me with challenges because He pours His Spirit into a broken vessel." She continued, "From that time to this moment, I sense His presence all the time."

She recalled several incidences that testify to the presence of the Holy Spirit in her life. She vividly remembered one night coming home from a mid-week church service. Sope and her brothers, Kehinde and Pelumi were with her. As they got off the bus to cross the road, she received a prompting of the Holy Spirit telling her to empty the money in her purse and leave only her Bible and tracts inside. She obeyed promptly. The boys walked briskly ahead to get home while their mom and sister walked slowly behind in the dark, quiet street. Suddenly, a man on a motorcyle headed towards Grace. She tried to get out of his way, but he forcefully grabbed her purse with her big Bible in it and quickly sped off. Fortunately, she still had her money and wristwatch which she had taken out earlier. Then the Holy Spirit told her not to shout after him as he could be caught and lynched. She felt God say to her, "Let him take the Bible away, I will meet him there." In those days, punishment for thieves was very severe, an instant death from a mob was likely. Grace felt the Lord had a plan for the thief's salvation. She misses that Bible but has had many others over the years. Her hope is that the man found the love of Christ through it. We listened as my mother spoke. The words were real and heartfelt, reflecting the grace of God. We asked her to share more of her encounters of God's presence. She responded that there were so many, but she had forgotten. She prayed to God to bring to her memory the ones He would want written down. Till today, she continues to affirm the faithfulness of His presence in her life.

On one occasion, she and her husband were invited to a birthday party of one of his relatives. She dressed up for the occasion and they both attended. The service was held at a church with the party following at the celebrant's house. As soon as they got back home she was about to remove her outfit when she heard, "Why did you go to that place? Don't go to such a place again. I know you are not aware of what is in that place. I covered you." She came to realize that He is a jealous God. At that, she knelt quickly and prayed. The Holy Spirit is very gentle indeed. As God, He humbled Himself to talk to dust - we humans. Imagine that! She continued, "Salvation is the story of GRACE! He makes you to know it's not by your ego."

She made reference to the Israelites when God took them out of Egypt into the Promised Land for their possession. They were not to conform to the ways of the people in the land but to know that He is a just and righteous God. This denotes an exodus from sin to repentance, darkness to light and from religion to relationship by the saving grace of Jesus. Grace explained that this was what happened to her that day. "I didn't know then. I now know, and I know He is everywhere. I give glory to His name. Who am I to speak of God, to speak of Jesus! Even angels tremble and won't speak His name. He is their King. He didn't die for them, He died for us. He forgave me." Her voice trembled as she extolled the greatness of God.

She reminded us that in John, it says there was no end to the stories of Jesus [7], and she couldn t possibly recall all her experiences in her journey with Him. As she spoke, she said the Holy Spirit had just brought to her mind a lady, who came to her with so many problems. She asked Grace why her own problems didn't overwhelm her. "It is all about Jesus. Let Him take hold of your life, I told her." Grace invited her to a crusade meeting where the lady gave her life to Jesus. She also recalled inviting her sister, Esther, to the revival meeting and she also gave her life to Jesus. "All glory be to God!" she exclaimed. "God saved me by His power, thank you Jesus! It is all for Him, not me, Grace, but God doing the work." As we continued with the session, my mother stated how it is important to know we can't handle challenges all by ourselves. "We have to give them to Christ and then He steps in and reveals Himself in the situation." Gradually, she learned to lean on Him after she gave her life to Him. "The taste of the pudding is always in the eating," she interjected. "He won't step in until you are faced with difficulties you can't solve, and you are desperate. A deeper walk comes through challenges," she said, citing the Bible story of Gideon who went to thresh wheat in desperate times. He had a divine encounter in the process where he confessed his fears and inadequacy.[8] Grace reminded us that the posture of humility and trust is important in our walk with God. Challenges brought wisdom, peace, victory and blessings because God showed up in every case. "He reminds me He wants to do something and that He will start and finish His work to His glory because it's not by might nor power but by His Spirit." [9]

Righteousness

Describing the way she feels about how God has led her in her relationship with Him, Grace stated, "I don't want to seem proud. Although He wants us to walk majestically and confidently with Him, I cannot in my own strength." She paused and continued, "I am humbled by what He has done for me. We need to learn to say, "Thank You, Papa God." She affirmed that neither money nor position could get or achieve what the Lord has done for her. She described Him as the One who turns sorrow into joy and moves in ways beyond what we can fathom to perform His wonders. She referred again to the story of Gideon where God told him to cut down the trees in his father's grove and use it to make a fire for a burnt offering to Him. When the people of the town came and saw their idol's trees cut down, they challenged Gideon and wanted to capture him, but his father responded with the counter-challenge that they should allow their idol to defend itself. "It is a great lesson which applies to us today," Grace stated. "There are things God needs to remove from our lives before He steps in. We have to learn to listen to Him – to that still small voice. We often don't want to do this. God can't share His glory with anyone." Asked if she would have done things differently, she exclaimed emphatically, "No, never! There is only one way and that is Jesus." She revealed that people tried to dissuade and distract her from her decision to follow Jesus wholeheartedly. They tried to interfere when God touched her life. She was accused of being a fanatic and to them, she had gone to the extreme in her faith. Through all this, she remained relentless. She always told them to let her take responsibility for the decision she had made.

"You have to release yourself from certain things if you want to follow Him." Before then, she loved to wear a lot of gold jewellery. Her siblings loved the heavy jewellery too, and perhaps coming from a royal line encouraged this. After her personal encounter with Jesus, Grace said God took away those desires from her. One day, she felt a strong sense of Him removing the heavy jewellery by an invisible tap. She remarked, "He didn't talk, but I felt

Him point to each piece instructing that it be taken off." She continued, "Jesus took those things away from my life to remove the enemy's power over me, Amen!" Although she felt isolated by her family, she always told them to leave her alone with God. She attests to His enduring faithfulness in her life. Though they also attended their different churches, she believed she needed Him most. "If it hadn't been Jesus Christ, Lord Almighty, where would I be?" She spoke with immense gratitude. "When you give all to Him, the enemy cannot hurt you."

Almost immediately, she recalled yet another incident that happened many years ago in Nigeria. Her son-in-law had dropped off one of the grandchildren at her house. As he was leaving, the Holy Spirit prompted her to call him back and pray for him. At first, she hesitated, but she was so thankful that God made her obey His prompting that day. She prayed for him that God would keep him safe. Grace recalled that it was a very short prayer and soon after, he left. As he drove through a guard of soldiers on the highway, he was stopped at gunpoint and forced out of his car with one of the soldiers pointing a gun directly at his head. It happened that they had mistaken him for one of the plotters of a coup that had happened in the country a couple of days before. To them, he resembled one of those who had escaped arrest. Fortunately, a superior officer who was watching from a distance, quickly gave an order to the soldier to stop the arrest. Her son-in law was finally let go after some questioning.

Grace said the experience always reminded her to listen to God and to know that He is always in control. She gives praise and thanks to Him for saving her. She saw herself as empty, not able to do anything to save herself, but He came to her rescue in His timely intervention which she cannot explain. "That is why I always give Him glory and adoration; honor and praise," she jubilated.

Gratitude

Grace expressed her gratitude to God for bringing her to Canada, saying the hand of the Lord guided her life and affairs. She likened her immigration to the biblical time when God brought the Israelites out of Egypt. He did that for her family for which she gives Him praise. She said He has put into her heart to continually say, "Thank You Jesus," adding that He has never failed her since.

She vividly described her experience when she first came to Canada. In those early days, she yearned to go back to Nigeria to continue to share God's Word in the environment she was used to. She didn't want to keep her salvation story to herself but wanted to continue to freely share what Christ had done in her life.

It was a different environment here. My sister Yemisi had told mom that she couldn't just go out on the street to speak about Jesus as she did in Nigeria. Grace continued to think of how she could share the love of God with people and give out Christian tracts. "The Holy Spirit then said to me, 'Don't worry, go and get a world globe. Put it in front of you and pray.'" Grace said He told her He would do His job as she prayed. He would save those He wanted to save. He told her not to go back to Nigeria as He had a purpose for her coming to Canada. Grace narrated how on the following Sunday, she saw a minister of God on television praying with a globe for the nations of the world! She was astounded. Since then she is not under any pressure to speak to people about God. She sees prayer as her passion. She encourages God's people to have an attitude of prayer, saying souls are being wasted and they need to come to the knowledge of Jesus. For this reason, she said we have a responsibility to continue on our knees more and more. "Our job is to raise up our hands and pray for mercy that God will show them their end so they can turn to Him." She continued, "He has already done the work. He has provided through Christ. This is our job now." She mentioned the recent terrorist attacks in France and other places in the world. "We need to be praying, 'Lord, save souls today! Have mercy Papa God.'"

Grace affirmed how it is because of God's mercy that we are pardoned and saved. We are not better than anyone else. So the work He has given us now is to pray and ask Him to make people everywhere aware. They must have spiritual insight about what He has already accomplished on the cross of Calvary and the salvation they have been freely given.

At this point in the session, Pam asked Grace to share her family's journey to Canada. "What led you here? and what outstanding thing came out of that?" she asked. She listened attentively and paused for a while. She then broke out in response with a song, "God will make a way, where there seems to be no way..." After her song she replied, "God Himself did it. We were all established in Nigeria, a big family and all was going well. But in God's eyes, He had some things ahead of us we didn't know, so He made a way for us to be here. Through my son-in-law and his wife, we began the process to come here." She mentioned how they thought it was going to be difficult for her daughter, Taiwo, to be here because of her developmental disability. Grace exclaimed, "God can stretch His hand and it is done! And as Jesus said, 'If you don't believe in me, believe in the works that I do."[10] She continued to recall the sequence of events that led to her and Taiwo's relocation.

Pelumi submitted the visa applications for her, Dad and Taiwo at the Canadian Embassy in Nigeria. They were scheduled to attend an interview prior to the issuance of their visas. The officer at the embassy had recognized the names and address on the applications. She knew the Macarthy family well, as her husband and Grace's son-in-law, Kola, had worked in the same local missions together. With the approval of her boss, the interview process was waived for all three. This was in April 2003.

Grace erupted into another song, "God moves in a mysterious way, His wonders to perform…" They had received their Canadian visas, and travel plans were also in place, when sadly, Dad passed away in May. Travelling had to be put on hold until after the funeral in June. In the midst of all this, there was a big national strike by the Labour Unions. There was a deadlock with the Federal government and everything was on shutdown. "We had only fifteen days till the visas expired in July. The workers refused to call off the strike and

and the government wasn't forthcoming as well." Grace recounted how one night, she woke up and raised up the visas and prayed, "Lord God almighty, You are the owner of heaven and earth, everything belongs to You. If it is Your will for us to go to Canada, it is in Your hand. The government and labor union are in a big strike, have mercy." She put the visas away and went back to sleep. Early in the morning, on a Tuesday, the strike was called off! Grace said she left it in His hands and He took over. "Papa God, Papa God, You did a miracle for Taiwo!" she exclaimed with a deep sense of joy and thankfulness. "God is a miracle-working God," she continued as she burst into song, "He's a miracle working God..." She sang again and again.

The process for Taiwo's stay began when she eventually arrived Canada with Grace. When the psychologist on the medical team was told that Taiwo was already in the country, he encouraged them to "fight on" on her behalf. "That is the work of God. Nothing is impossible for Him. She is here because of God's provision," Grace remarked.

Grace shared that the Bible is her favourite

book and how she had received an instruction from God to read His Word. "This Word belongs to God. It represents Him. If you take it by faith and obey and follow the narrow way, His desire for you and I will be made real." Grace continued, "We cannot see God, but through His Word, you feel His touch, His love, His presence, His victory throughout your life on this earth till you go to the other side." She affirmed that God's Word represents Him and the Holy Spirit is the guide. And to fulfil His Word, He shed His blood for the remission of the sin of humanity. She described the Bible as the book of God's power. "It is not a story book and it can meet every need of humankind," she spoke emphatically.

Confidence

Grace's constant desire is for God to use her as a lighthouse to others in His will to help them find the right way to follow. She prays that at the end of the journey, He will make His home her home, saying, "The Word says if you are living only for this world, you are the most miserable of men."[11]

As she spoke, my mother recalled an accident she had over four years ago in the house: she had fallen in the shower and broke her leg. An ambulance was called right away to transport her to the hospital. It happened that I was on my sister's street at the same time taking a driving lesson. I stopped when I saw the ambulance, parked outside the house, and told my driving instructor I had to find out what was happening. It was then I learned that my mother had a fall. I got into the ambulance with her as we headed to the hospital, while my sister and her husband joined us later. After the surgery, she was in intensive care for two weeks, not talking or eating. After two more weeks at the hospital, she was discharged and transferred to a senior's nursing home for mobility rehabilitation where she stayed for another month.

Grace described the incident as a difficult time but thanked God for His intervening power. She recalled a day during her stay at the nursing home when the lady she shared a room with asked her what she was reading. She replied that it was her Bible. The lady then asked her family to bring in a Bible and from then on, they both shared God's Word together. She would sing praise songs each morning and the other patients always wanted her to sing for them in the mornings. Remarkably, she soon forgot about the pains in her leg and enjoyed the opportunity to share her faith with others. She confidently spoke of the reality of God's Word and the guidance of His Spirit in her life. Grace finds strength, courage, victory and peace through His Word. She loves to sing because God gave her a passion for singing. She praises Him and declares His Word through songs. She recalled that when Jesus was tempted in the wilderness by the devil, He used the Word of God, by the power of the Holy Spirit to cause him to flee.

Conviction

Mom narrated three significant episodes of temptation she was faced with in her pastoral ministry years ago in Nigeria. The first happened in the early years. "It was a temptation," Grace recounted, "It is not a sin to be tempted, but when you follow through, it is a sin." She recounted how she had been busy with church engagements and decided to take a personal break for three days. On the Sunday that followed, during the service, an usher came to her to say there was someone outside who wanted to see the head pastor. She went with the usher to the parking lot where three men were waiting in a Mercedes Benz. They wanted to leave a package in the church till the following Tuesday. Opening the car trunk, they brought out a suitcase with money which they hinted was sixty-three million American dollars. They implored her to keep it safe for them as they knew she was a minister of God and would not double-cross them and promised to give her a percentage of it.

They opened the suitcase and insisted it wasn't fake money. She touched it, and the pile of notes felt warm. She received a prompting of the Holy Spirit in her heart that the money was stolen. Grace looked sternly at the three men and beckoned them to come closer. Taking her Bible from the usher standing nearby she began to admonish them, "God's Word says, 'he who steals cannot enter the Kingdom of God.' Take this money back to where you got it from. It is not your money. Jesus said you are to work with your hands and let it satisfy you." Nervously, the men entered their car and quickly drove out of the church premises.

In another incident at church, Grace had been fasting and praying, and while waiting for her husband to pick her up, a visitor came to see the senior pastor. He had a bag of money and asked her to keep it till the following Monday. This time it was British pounds. "Take this back! A thief will never enter the Kingdom of God. Work with your hands and be satisfied," she rebuked. Like the others, he promised her a portion of the money but again she turned down the offer stating that she didn't need it.

The third incident happened when she was in her house in Falolu Street. It was a rainy day she recalled. The doorbell rang, and on her doorstep stood a caucasian with three other men. They explained how they had twenty million Nigerian naira in the suitcase and knew they could trust her to look after it. Irate at such a request, she pointed at the police post next door to her house and threatened to call the police if they didn't leave immediately.

"It was indeed a great temptation," Grace confessed. But God took her through it and proved Himself strong on her behalf. "Without Christ, you are in crisis. Christ too was tempted, and he answered by the Word. The enemy is a liar and deceiver," she remarked.

It was a full day. The session ran a little longer than planned but filled with many recollections of Mother's experience on her faith journey. We tucked in to the light refreshments my sister had provided during our short breaks. Mom's spontaneous outbursts of praise songs were the highlights of the day. It felt like we were at a choir practice! Her heartfelt songs affirmed God's presence. Truly He gave her this passion for singing!

Pam had more questions for Grace. She asked what significant compliment or honor she had received in Nigeria or Canada over the years. Grace replied that she was given an honorary doctorate in Nigeria by the late Pastor J.O. Martins, the founder and senior pastor of the Free Gospel Centre (now known as Winners Gospel Centre), under whom she served for over twenty-five years in the church. This honor was conferred on her in recognition of her spiritual call and service in the Gospel of Christ. The apostle Paul confirms that no one takes this honor by himself except given by the Lord.[12] Grace ascribed the glory to God. She revealed that He had been with her from youth even though she didn't know she offended Him, He didn't leave her: "He says all have sinned and come short of the glory of God. It is true. He spoke in the garden that if mankind ate from the tree He told them not to, they would surely die. That is where the troubles of humanity came from – the rebellion at the Garden." She added, "We have to humble ourselves under the throne of God." Grace continues to attest to God's presence as the greatest impact and influence in her life before and after she knew the Lord personally.

She went on to tell us a story about herself which her mother had told her. When she was two years old, her parents lived in a large family house with different apartments which were rented out. A man, who would later be her father-in-law also lived in the same building. She would walk, taking baby steps to his apartment, and he would always welcome her and say that Grace would marry his son. She was only a toddler. Though it seemed unreal then, it happened many years later just as he predicted. The story was an amusing one, but could it possibly be a coincidence or a divine plan? It does make one wonder.

Grace continued, "God had His hand on me even then. That's why I cannot compromise. Christ gets all the glory." Mother's memory raced back again to when she was a child of three or four years. From time to time young children in the area would be kidnapped and killed for ritual purposes, in their abductor's quest for money, power or fame. As Grace was outside playing with her friends, some unknown men grabbed her. It was a terrifying experience. The abductors took her and some other children to a house which was very dark inside. They were stripped of their clothing and lined up in a room, and then taken one after the other to another room where they were decapitated. When it came to her turn, the doorkeeper gave her back her clothes and sent her out of the house. She doesn't remember how she got back home to her family who were frantically searching for her that night. God's grace was especially with her even then.

Encouragement

Grace referred to her mother, Celina, fondly called Mama Agba, (older mother), as the person who had the greatest impact in her life. Her mother's legacy of faith was an unwavering example of godly virtue that she embraced and nurtured in her own life also. She mentioned that her mother was instrumental in her decision to personally give her life to Jesus. Pam asked, "What life lessons did you learn from your mother and how have you learned to give and receive this grace?" Grace narrated how her mother was a profound example to her and whom she said demonstrated a life of faith in Christ expressed in practical ways. One way that stands out to Grace was her commitment to caring and giving to others within her resources and being a rallying point for many for physical, emotional or financial needs. This same virtue was passed on to Grace as she learned the joy of preparing and sharing dishes and delicacies from her kitchen, lighting up a face with a smile, encouraging with words of wisdom, taking a posture of prayer, patiently nursing to health, passionately giving out Christian tracts, supporting and honoring with her purse; these are just some of the ways she too lives this lifestyle passed on from her mother. This heart of giving stems from an understanding that through Jesus, we are new creatures, God's masterpiece empowered to do good works that He planned for us to do long ago for His glory.[13] Caring and serving gives significance to life and stems from God's nature. When we learn to give, we express His character and that produces a positive impact on others and ourselves.

As she spoke, Grace mentioned the late Pastor Joseph Martins whom she always addressed as "Papa Martins", as someone from whom she also learned much about the grace of God. He had greatly encouraged her in the ways of God. "He would always share the Gospel in prayer and in his teachings of God's Word. He was a life example of how to live in the way God wanted." She also spoke of the times when she was able to extend grace to others. She quickly added that opportunities sometimes came with challenges and resistance from the enemy because he does not want people to know that "Christ is the Light of the world." God always helped her to overcome, and to share His message and give glory to Him. There was an optometrist who had his office close to her house in Falolu and one day she had an appointment to replace her glasses. While there, he suddenly reached out to her and told her that as she was speaking, he felt a healing occur in his body. He seemed unsteady and she helped him into a chair and prayed for him. She laid her hand on him as she prayed, and he recovered. "He nearly died, but God healed him," Grace narrated.

About a week later she received a call that her new glasses were ready. He looked so much better when she saw him, and to her surprise, he declined payment. She thanked him and happily left with her brand new glasses.

Grace spoke of her greatest fear and hope: "God, let me not depart from You, neither You depart from me." Her hope she affirmed, "is to gain Heaven and to let His hand of mercy be upon me." She continued, "I am thankful to God because His experience in my life is inexpressible." She likened it to the experience when the Lord met Peter when he didn't catch any fish. Christ told him to cast his net on the right side of the boat. "At Your Word Lord."

Peter responded.[14] "It is His command, His love, His mercy and not me. And him who thinks he can stand alone should beware," Grace added. Her happiest moment she revealed "is the day the Lord met me. Just as He told Peter to strengthen his brethren when he is restored,[15] I pray that whoever reads what is recorded in this biography will never be the same in the name of Jesus." She continued, "He is writing it to show His power, love, mercy and concern for humans – all thanks to Jesus, He is Lord and Savior."

Speaking about the frustrations and successes in her life, she candidly revealed that her daughter, Taiwo, who has a developmental disability has been of much concern to her over the years. "God said He didn't make her for this world but ultimately for the other side, for Heaven," she revealed. "I asked Him why, but He said, 'Leave it for now. It is for the other side.'" Grace explained that God's response to her concerning her daughter is what gives her joy even in the midst of the challenge. And she continues to find comfort and peace holding on to His Word for as long as she lives.

Grace remarked that God has been her strength. She is an industrious woman who always kept the family moving. She saw her role as a housewife as a profession and always trusted the Lord for His grace and strength. One day, she was coming from church and decided to do some grocery shopping on her way home. She walked through the Lagos University Teaching Hospital which was one of her usual routes home carrying her shopping bags. As she walked, a Mercedes Benz pulled up beside her. The driver, a young man, offered to give her a ride home and took her bags and put them in the trunk. She didn't recognize him, but he recognized her. It happened that she had witnessed Christ to him and his friend when they were still medical students at the hospital. Some years had passed, and they were now doctors. She was amazed at his memory and she didn't know what to say as she was in awe of the goodness of God.

"If you are aware of God's mercy to you, you need to be careful about people provoking your spirit," Grace said. "You need to guard what God has put in you, so you won't be discouraged or distracted from your course," she added. When she is confronted or insulted without reason, she would rather choose to pray for her offenders than say anything to them. "If they did it to my Savior, let them insult me," she said. She sees it as something she must pass through, as a trial to test her faith. Asked if she would do things differently in her life, Grace responded that if things aren't according to what God wants, she will never cooperate.

Covenant

It was a week since the last interview. A warm Friday afternoon, Pam and I were back. We got there as planned, and immediately started off the session with my mother. "What are some lessons God has taught you over the years in your personal life, family, career and ministry?" Pam asked. Grace responded that her personal relationship with Christ had taught her that He surrendered His life so that humanity can be restored. "That is His purpose and this work of restoration continues in a life He has touched till the end of that life on earth." She went further to explain that it is the work of the Holy Spirit to begin the good work in a life as the old nature must die. "You can't take an old cloth to patch a new one and you can't put new wine in an old skin or it will break," she spoke as she paraphrased Jesus' words.[16] The Holy Spirit who personifies the power of God reminds her that "the power of man can do nothing." This is a core lesson she has learned in life. Grace is thankful to God that He invited her family to Himself and stepped into their lives. She can't explain or comprehend it, but as she looks at her children, and sees Him giving them the victory no matter what they are passing through, it reminds her that Christ is alive. "He is the doer of His work," she remarked.

Grace recalled her earlier years as a fashion designer. When she was on the sewing machine, she gave full concentration to the upper part of the machine, where she directed the stitches on the fabric with her hands and with her foot, at the same time, pressing on the lower motor. She would not look at the motor but was focused on monitoring the stitches on the cloth. She mentioned that God reminded her of those days, and gave her that analogy to teach her of His sovereignty. He helped her understand that He is in control and that she shouldn't look around to people or things but give her attention to Him. Christ always gave her the ability to endure any condition He allowed. He helped her focus her attention on Him as she shared the Good News with others, and they were never the same again. "Through the power of the Holy Spirit, it is forward ever, backward never," Grace declared joyfully with a big smile on her face. She continued, "It is not an easy road, but it becomes easy when we focus on Him." As usual, she broke into song, "I have decided to follow Jesus. No looking or turning back."

After singing, she paused for a little while, then began to tell the story of a man she met in Ajegunle, a notoriously rough neighbourhood in the city. The church had visited the place for an outreach, and it happened that the young man named Blessing, gave his life to Jesus. "God is no respecter of persons, He poured His Spirit on him," Grace narrated. "Remember, we're all going to be tested. When you pass, He will promote you. This young man after some time of being encouraged and nurtured in his new faith, went back to his old ways." Many months had gone by, and Blessing wasn't coming to fellowship any more. One day, he came to visit Grace. When she saw him, she asked what was wrong. He felt empty. He couldn't eat or sleep. She instructed him to meet her at church later. Everyone noticed he wasn't himself. She told him to go to the altar where he began to pray and weep. Grace said the Holy Spirit prompted, "Fear God, tell him to stand up and go take a bath." He went to the church's bathroom and took a bath. When he returned, his countenance had changed because the glory of God had been restored to him. Blessing's story resonated with the story of the prodigal son [17] in which the relationship was restored between father and son. God restored the young man's relationship with Him. "God came to preserve life and not to destroy it. That's how Blessing came back. He was used by God to take the Gospel to his town outside Lagos, and he was a blessing." She yet affirmed that only God can equip a person by the power of the Holy Spirit. It is not what one can do. She gives Him all the glory for using her as a vessel to reveal His supernatural ability in the lives of others saying, "When He shows mercy, it is not because you qualify for it, it calls for humility," she concluded.

Grace continued to recall the different encounters and experiences in her life while serving Christ and serving the community. These have continued to make an impact in her life and in others', affirming God's presence and power in ways He chooses to reveal it. She remembered an instance many years ago in Nigeria. Her church had planned a crusade at the outskirts of the city. They were on their way to the location and she was scheduled to preach there. As she travelled with some ministers on the bus, she was shown a local newspaper that ran the story of someone who lived to be 140 years old. When she saw it, she put down the story and remarked she would not want to live that long. They got to the crusade ground and hundreds of people were already there. The service started and went on until she was being introduced to come to the podium. Suddenly, she realized she couldn't stand up from her seat. Her hands and legs felt lifeless. She quickly prayed, "Papa God, what is happening?" Almost immediately she was reminded of her disbelief on the bus that anyone could live so long. She asked God for forgiveness, and she immediately felt normal in her hands and legs again. She walked to the podium and gave the message, and testified to the outpouring of His love, mercy, and power at the crusade. She said, "God's concern for His work is so great and though we all fall short, nevertheless, He came to give us abundant life."

She was in England a few years ago on vacation, in her son's house. While she was still in bed one morning, she heard a knock on the bedroom door. She knew no one was home, everyone had gone to work. Suddenly she heard a voice saying, "I AM," causing her to bow in prayer. Later when everyone got back home she told them what happened. Remarkably, a day before we arrived for this interview session, her son, Kenny, had called from London to share a similar experience he had. Grace was thankful she had told him then. "That is why we share our testimonies. It's not your own doing," Grace spoke and broke out into song: "Somebody touched me…when I was praying."

Grace recalled an incident that happened many years ago in Nigeria. Some ministers gathered every Wednesday, to pray for revival. After some time, one of them stopped attending the meetings. This lady was a commercial farmer with workers on her large farm. One day, a big snake circled behind her as she was on her farm, but she didn't know. The Holy Spirit told her to look behind her, and she saw the snake. He told her if she ran suddenly, that would be her end. She was to start praising God! After about thirty minutes of praise, the snake finally left. "What is man that You are mindful of him," Grace exclaimed quoting the psalmist.
[18] Thursdays were usually when time was given to share testimonies in the church. The minister

got on the pulpit to share her encounter at the farm. "He sometimes puts us in difficult places to recognize that He is in control, not us!" Grace said.

Grace has a lot of Bible verses and passages she often reads. She mentioned that among others, her favourite verses are: 2 Chronicles 7:14, John 3:16, John 10:10, Genesis 45:26. The latter is the story of Joseph when his brothers told Jacob that his son was still alive. He was stunned beyond measure and his spirit revived. Grace added that the verse has a profound meaning in her life. "Only God can revive us. Whatever man can do to you, God can turn it around to bring glory to His name." I interjected with another favourite passage of Scripture mom often shared. It was the experience of the two disciples on the road to Emmaus after the resurrection of Jesus.[19] She remarked that the hymn *Abide with me* [20] was inspired by the encounter the disciples had with Jesus. "He knows everything, especially our frailty," she said. "He speaks, no matter how frail we are. His Spirit revives. When He speaks, life comes forth. They didn't recognize Him, they thought He was a stranger. He opened up the Scriptures to them."

Another favourite verse is Acts 1:8, "Wait until you are endued with power from above." Only by the power of the Holy Spirit can we show God's love and forgiveness to others, Grace explained. She also mentioned Revelation 3:18 saying we are to ask for cloth to cover our nakedness and salve for our eyes to see. She included Psalm 50:19-23 as another often-read Scripture. Her favourite Scriptures wouldn't be complete without John 19:30 when Jesus said on the cross, "It is finished!" She revealed that this verse was prompted in her by the Holy Spirit. Its personal significance to her is that it reveals her year of birth and that the Lord has declared that all her pain and sorrows are finished. It was amazing when she shared this with me a few years ago. Sometime after then, I called her as I was prompted by the Holy Spirit and told her the verse also has the numbers of her birthday month and day. A divine plan of His grace, one could say!

We went on with the session as Pam indicated that the Bible says that there are different kinds of spiritual gifts or special abilities that the Holy Spirit gives to believers for different kinds of service.[21] Grace vividly recalled an incident that occurred on her way back from

Nigeria after a visit. "I was sitting at the edge of a row of chairs at the airport lounge in Lagos in 2015," she narrated. "A man was there, and he was looking very sick. Suddenly I heard, "'That man is sick. Tell him he will not die. I will heal him if he repents.'" At her request, Grace said God confirmed the words she heard. Immediately, the man's wife came and sat beside him. She opened her purse and Grace saw a Bible inside. "I saw that as a sign from Papa God. I beckoned to her and she came to me and knelt. I told her the message – God will heal him (her husband) if he confesses his sin and repents. He had a problem in his intestines," Grace narrated. By the time Grace left the airport lounge, the atmosphere with that family had changed for the better.

"We cannot know what God can do because of His unfathomable nature. He knows us more than ourselves," she said. She doesn't feel worthy of operating in this gift of the "word of knowledge"[22] which she attributes to the presence of the Holy Spirit. She quickly made reference to Ezekiel's encounter with God in the valley of dry bones[23] saying, "Everything He gives us, we give Him back." The Holy Spirit also works through her in the gift of healing by "the laying on of hands."[24] Grace affirmed this as she paraphrased from the Bible, "Concerning the works of my hands, command ye Me."[25]

Grace has spent many years preaching and teaching God's Word. She remarked that when people come to Jesus, they have an expectation of receiving from Him. She broke into a song, "You won't leave here as you came in Jesus name…." – one of the songs she usually sang when ministering to people. "You put yourself under Him and His Word, you are not the one doing it. He is the owner of His work. Recognize this and put yourself under the control of the Holy Spirit," she said. "You are just the postman and not the one to open the letter; you just deliver!" she added humorously.

Pam mentioned the nine fruits of the Holy Spirit. She asked Grace to describe how important they are for Christian growth. Her response was that a spiritual gift is given to a person at the discretion of the Holy Spirit. The fruit on the other hand, puts a divine responsibility on a believer to cultivate and develop it. "We do not live alone, we live and interact with people and we have to learn to tolerate others. We can't do that unless by the Spirit of God," she explained. She spoke further, "We are to pray for our enemies, and we cannot do that unless He gives us the grace. Love, Joy, Peace, Patience, Kindness, Goodness, Faithfulness, Gentleness and Self Control all come from the Holy Spirit. Holy Spirit, thank You! It is the thief that comes to steal and destroy," Grace added.

She recalled a day she was returning from a church service. It was raining, and she was wet and cold. It was a great test for her that day. She was almost home, and she could sense the enemy was trying to fill her mind with the hurts her husband had done to her in the past. It was true. She heard the whisper, "Are you going to greet him, considering all he has done to you?" "I didn't answer," she said. As soon as she got home and saw her husband who had opened the door, she greeted him well as was the custom. The devil wanted to steal her joy; he had reminded her word for word what her husband had done to her. "We will be tested," Grace remarked. She continued, "Why? That is because, without examination you cannot be promoted. Every challenge is to test, so you can have the confidence of the Holy Spirit to testify about His love, power and presence." She further explained, "You can't take three steps at a time. You will hurt yourself! Jesus gives enough examples of His own life that we can emulate. 'Why call Me Lord if you refuse to do what I ask?' You walk according to His Word. It is hard, but He is the Helper."

Early years of Grace and Robert as a couple

Grace & Robert's Wedding Day - April 17, 1952

Grace at Trafalgar Square, London - 1958

Top (L -R): Toyin, Robert, Grandma Celina carrying Pelu, Grace, and Rotimi. Bottom (L to R): Yemisi, Kenny, Sope, Taiwo, and Bisi (Oto)

Robert and Grace at one of their children's engagement

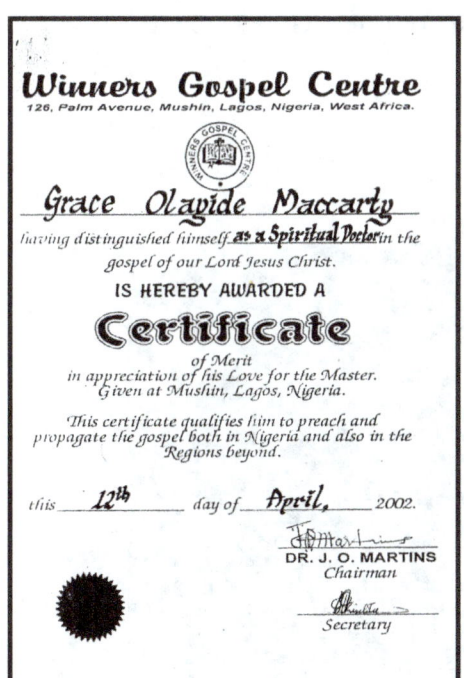

Certificate of Honor given to Grace Macarthy in recognition of Kingdom service.

Robert as a delegate in the Nigerian Wrestling Association

Grace during her ministry days at Winners Gospel Centre

Family house at 39, Falolu Street, Lagos.

Papa Robert O. Macarthy
as Captain of the Boys' Brigade
of the Mainland Battalion

Ambassador

Grace spoke extensively of her ministry work both in Nigeria and Canada. When she was in Nigeria, she was often invited to preach in churches and at crusades. She vividly and humorously recalled a time she was to preach at a crusade. She prepared her message from the Bible and had it written down. She got to the podium to speak and all of a sudden, her mind went blank. She couldn't remember anything she wrote. "I will never forget it to this day!" she exclaimed and continued. "Prepare what you want to say and put it in His presence. He is the owner of the Word; let Him take over." Grace said the Lord told her, "I am your Scripture, open your mouth and I will fill it." And just as He said, He filled her mouth. She broke into a song as she continued her story. That day at the crusade service, she witnessed people touched by God in healings and restoration of lives. "It is more than I can say," she said emphatically. "He knows them. He knows the problems. When you stand before His people, you humble yourself, give glory to Him and He does the work and receives the glory."

Grace's church ministry in Nigeria started with the Prayer team. She also served with the Outreach team for door to door evangelism and city crusades and missions. She was part of the ushering team for about three years and gradually over the years, became an ordained minister in the church. These transitions from one area of service to another were gradual. Grace explained that growth isn't automatic or immediate. It is the same for spiritual growth and maturity. It is one step and then, another. "Before He promotes you to a higher level, you must spend time in the class," she said. She continued, "God is patient in helping us to grow and it is systematic. If there is something not of Him, He will correct, teach and lead you; He does not rush!" she added jokingly. Through the process, she sees His hand giving her opportunities. With Grace's usual pauses to sing, she burst into a song. "It is not I that lives, but Christ that lives in me."

In Canada, God instructed her to pray for the nations. She initially wanted to go back to Nigeria to continue His work there. Now she is encouraged to pray for the nations of the world that they would know He is the Light. She pointed to the world globe she keeps in her room, which she brought downstairs with her Bible for the session. It was inspiring to see Grace's commitment to praying for the nations. Since coming to Canada in 2003, she has attended Pickering Pentecostal Church, on Bayly Street in Pickering. She mentioned how she has been blessed spiritually by the various pastoral leaderships of the church since then till now.

Presently, Grace is involved with the senior's group in the church. "We sing, share our experiences with one another and intercede in prayer," she said. The group also has lots of eating time together and go on field trip. Grace's son-in-law, Kola, often takes her to the meetings. A similar experience to these meetings that came to mind as my mother shared her experiences was way back in Nigeria. It brings back exciting memories in her Christian journey over the many years in fellowship with others which encouraged her faith. They would have night vigils once every month from 11pm to 3am, and every first Monday to Wednesday of the month would be set aside for fasting and praying. The ministers involved included Pastors Akinmojesu,

Jesugbamila, Taiwo, Olaolu, Grace Akiode and my mother, Grace Macarthy. During the days of fasting they would all meet each day in church and pray together. The last day was when my mother would prepare lots of food from home and take it to church to share with themselves. They would particularly look forward to the delicious dishes she would bring. Others also brought fruits, snacks and drinks to share. The fasting would then be rounded up with great feasting to the delight of everyone! She recalled how it was always a joyful time spent together.

As we wrapped up the session, Pam asked my mother to describe the cultural change she experienced when she immigrated to Canada. Listening to Grace's experiences of life in Nigeria sparked Pam's interest in a culture so vibrant yet different from the Canadian culture. My mother leaned forward, and with her hands rested on the table, she pulled herself closer to us for a clearer view. With calmness in her voice, she responded, "I would say there's no culture in Jesus' Kingdom."

She continued, "We are to love each other, give support as needed to others and let them know that Christ is Lord. It is not just about our human cultures, but it should be Kingdom culture that reflects unity in diversity."

Grace mentioned that though there are practical differences in cultures, the emphasis must be His culture, saying, "Hope gives redemption to any culture - this hope is Jesus! Let His Spirit lead, guide and orchestrate things for you – that is His culture!" We all had a good laugh at this as we called it a day. Grace had the opportunity to visit Nigeria again in 2007 and 2015. The church at Christ Harvest Centre, London, England has also been blessed by Grace's ministry through God's word and prayer whenever she visits her children there.

Counsel

A cool and decently warm Sunday in July, Pam and I planned to conclude the sessions today. The drive was quiet and smooth as the roads were free from the bustle of a weekday. We arrived there at about two in the afternoon. My nephew, Toni, opened the door and welcomed us in. His mom also came from the kitchen with a warm smile on her face, and ushered us further into their home.

We walked into the main living room, where my mother was seated, waiting. In a beautiful floral blouse, she greeted us with excitement as we exchanged hugs. We began our way to the usual spot in the dining area and quickly settled in, ready to start the session.

We began by asking what it was that gave Grace the peace she walked in. She took a deep breath and paused to gather her thoughts before she responded. She shared how after she invited Jesus into her life, He gradually began to let her know His nature and form it in her life through an ongoing process. She affirmed that He gives her peace: anytime, anywhere, she feels His presence and it reminds her that He is at work. "To know Him is to know His mercy and love," she added. Like Queen Esther in the Bible, Grace said God protects her no matter what the situation and stands by her just as He stood with Esther. She expressed thankfulness to Him for His love, guidance and direction and said He even wakes her up sometimes at night to praise Him. "I am content with His presence, He gives me joy, happiness and peace," Grace remarked. She went further to recall the story of Jesus calming the storm.[26] "With his disciples in the boat, He was there fast asleep. They were in trouble desperately trying to get water out of the boat in their human wisdom. He was testing them," she explained. With the story, she pointed out that true peace is found in Jesus, and that when people come to the cross, He is always there. She broke into song as she spoke, "In the cross, in the cross, be my glory ever, till my ransomed soul shall find rest beyond the river."[27] Grace used the analogy of a child starting school to describe growth and maturity in walking with Christ. "The child won't understand everything immediately, but as he or she attends school daily and listens to the teacher, they will learn and grow." Grace continued, "The day you give your life to Jesus, you are enrolled in God's academy. You are a newcomer in His class, and you receive the same uniform as Christ."

Like good students, Pam and I listened attentively as Grace painted a picture with her words to describe our relationship with the Lord. It was beautiful. She added that Psalm 119 reminds us we are to take His Word each day, little by little and grow in His love and grace while "looking unto Jesus, the author and finisher of our faith."[28] "We have no friend like Him," Grace affirmed. "Nothing can ever miss His eye. Before He gives you a question, He knows the answer, and He helps us to stand firm by His grace which results in promotion for you. It moves you forward. Satan can't do anything where Christ reigns, that is the bottom line. Immediately you have Christ's name, you are out of his net," Grace explained. She revealed that since Jesus saved her, she has nothing to fear, even death, because "You will live again, so don't trample on His blood but hear His beckoning voice today, for He's the owner of your soul," she concluded.

Grace has had a lot of memorable travel experiences. She recalled the many evangelistic trips to Ota on the outskirts of Lagos which I sometimes made with her during my teen years. She has made several trips to England on vacation. This year, she travelled to New York, visited Marine Land at Niagara Falls and Toronto Island with my sister, Yemisi and her family. We continued our conversation with Grace and she recalled one of the funniest things that ever happened to her.

Back in Nigeria, she would sometimes go out for personal evangelism. One evening, she went out, well dressed for evangelism. She walked the streets sharing Christian tracts. When she got to an intersection, a man in his car stopped and asked her to join him. She quickly brought out a tract from her purse, stretched it out to him at the passenger window and said, "Excuse me sir, Jesus loves you." At that he was turned off, and sped away, but not without the tract in his car! There was a burst of laughter as we imagined the disappointment the man had, but in retrospect, it could have been a divine appointment that changed the course of his life.

As a socialite, whose father was a renowned king, Grace's salvation experience couldn't be comprehended by her wider family, but she uncompromisingly stood her ground. "Many of them eventually gave their lives to Christ as the change they saw in me was so drastic," she remarked. It was another of the happiest memories of her life. She burst out with a song, "I have decided to follow Jesus, no turning back." Grace recalled yet another joyous occasion. It was at the wedding of one of her children.

The food at the reception was prepared in packages for the guests. There were so many people that attended, and the servers wondered if Grace realized how many people there were. They worried the food might not be enough. To their amazement, each time they came back for more food to serve, they discovered there was more than enough. "They had never experienced such a thing. The more food they served, the more food remained," she narrated. "It was Sope's wedding and no one knew where the food came from!" She exclaimed, her face lighting up in amusement. During church service the next day, some of the guests present at the wedding gave testimonies in praise to what God had done.

Grace is very proud of being saved out of the world. She is very thankful to God that He didn't let her go with the world. "Jesus said, 'what will it profit a man if he gains the world and loses his soul', I have nothing to be proud of in myself and I want to give Him glory to my last breath," Grace said. when asked Who her hero is; Grace excitedly responded, "The Holy Ghost is my biggest hero, He is alive forever!" She broke into a song almost immediately, "Holy Ghost fire fall on me as in the day of Pentecost." When she was done singing, she spoke of her deep desire to see greater transformation in the world. If she could change something in the world right now, her desire would be to see many "Sauls" turned to "Pauls" like the dramatic encounter of Saul with Jesus on his way to Damascus.[29] "That power is the same today and forever. That's what I would ask God to do for me; to soften hardened hearts and bring the prodigals back home," Grace's face became sombre as her voice wobbled with emotion. She strongly desires God's supernatural power to be revealed in the lives of people. She also drew a parallel from the life of the Syrian captain, Naaman, who received supernatural intervention in his life and afterwards took some soil from the land of Israel back to his country to remind him of the power and mercy of God.[30]

The story of another leper who had a transforming

encounter with Jesus came next as Grace spoke of her deep desire to see lives touched by God. The leper was hesitant in his request to be healed by Jesus saying, "If You will, you can make me clean." Grace remarked that Jesus' response was an absolute approval, "I am willing. Be healed!"[31] Grace continued insistently, "I want Him to do this for me. I want to see lives touched: new people, new marriages, and new families; wherever they are, 'Jesus, please intervene in their lives and situations.'" She revealed how God has given His people the grace and passion to call on Him for intervention, but if we don't call on the Lord, many will be lost eternally.

In 1979, Grace was in England to visit Toyin, her eldest daughter. During her stay, she didn't give out tracts on the streets, but gave them to visitors who came to her daughter's house. She had been quietly asking the Lord about the people of that nation in her prayers. One night, she had a dream. In that dream, there were many people who looked as though they represented the country's authorities dressed in their different regalia. They asked her who gave her the authority to come and preach there. "I was afraid," Grace confessed. She continued, "Before I could respond to them, the heavens opened, and a strong wind blew down a scroll to earth. It came between me and them. They caught a glimpse of what was written on it, and with fear on their faces, they ran away. Heaven intervened immediately!" She concluded her story with another song, "I'm not alone, in all my journey, Jesus is with me."

As a matriarch, Grace had words of wisdom for her posterity. She is so thankful that her children are living for Christ. She spoke with conviction and passion of her faith in Christ and His love and faithfulness in her life's journey. "This is why He is orchestrating these interviews. He is for me, and He's given me this opportunity to share what He has done for me," she said. Her remark resonates with the psalmist's words.[32] Grace paused, took a deep breath, her hands clasped, and continued, "My words and prayer to them would be to receive Him (Jesus) as Lord and Savior. There is no other way. You can't have treasure without Him." She paused to gather her thoughts. "Don't rely on yourself, cling to the cross, He will see you through. Whatever you are passing through, I assure you, He is a faithful God. Only believe, all things are possible. He says, 'Without Me, you can't do anything, but with Me, everything is possible.'"

Grace shared how she advises her grandchildren and prays for them not to be distracted in the journey of life. She used the parallel of Jesus when He prayed to the Father to keep the present and future generations that would come to believe in Him.[33] She spoke further using the words of Jesus, "I am the Vine, you are the branches."[34] She declared that fruitfulness in every way would come because nourishment is received from Him regularly and timely. She assured that if one is in Christ, "He will see that you are covered and that the enemy will have no power over you." She concluded with these words: "the world is full of darkness. And when Christ came to the world, no one recognized Him as God Almighty. However, when one comes to Him, He knows and understands you and your prayers." Grace also referred to Solomon's prayer when he dedicated the temple he built for God.[35] In a greater context however, no longer does God dwell in temples made with human hands. He desires to reveal His presence through the indwelling of the Holy Spirit in human temples.[36]

In this later stage of life, Grace looks forward to every day and every minute with the knowledge that God gives her strength. "Every day brings us closer to our real home," she said. She continued, "I keep busy with prayer and reading God's Word.

I worship and thank Him for the past, present and for His promises. I thank Him for everything He has done and believe He is going to do something greater." With a tone of excitement, she added quickly, "I say 'wow!' to His plans!" Grace's work now as she faces the future is to worship, adore and appreciate what He has done and let the world know He is alive, and that He is the only One who can set the captives free. She broke into a song as she spoke, "Jesus knows all about our sorrow, He will guide till the day is done, there's not a friend like the lowly Jesus, no not one."

Grace enjoys watching WWE on television, a sport her late husband also very much enjoyed. Her favourite channel is Sportsnet 360, on Mondays and Saturdays, where she watches wrestling matches. She even prays for them as they wrestle, because she believes some of them are believers too. Some, she said, carry a symbol of the cross on themselves, and when they win their fight, they point up, which to Grace indicates that they give God the glory! Out of all the wrestlers, Grace's favourite is John Cena, whose slogan is *Never Give Up*. She follows his matches closely and keeps him in her prayers. Grace loves gardening and gives her time to tending her vegetables and flowers during the summer months. It's the living of life in the total man – spirit, soul and body as God designed it. It is using the resources at our disposal to walk in wisdom for life in all aspects.

As we continued the session, Pam asked, "What do you see now when you look at yourself in the mirror? Have your goals and dreams changed through your life?" As though she knew the question was coming, my mother without hesitation answered, "My image in the mirror now tells me we are not to live here forever but there is a place for us forever." She continued, "Aging shouldn't bother Christians because we know Christ our Master, and the flesh is only temporary because our souls are immortal, and have a permanent home in heaven. We must not be afraid. I was in my room watching a TV program called, 'How it's made.' This particular episode was on making caskets." Grace revealed that when she saw the one she really liked, she said, "Papa God, I like this one." the Lord told her not to worry or be anxious about tomorrow. She added, "In your old age, God can do anything as in the life of Sarah. God quickens us by His Spirit."

Grace's expectations have remained the same. He encourages her and doesn't let her faith waver. He takes care of everything and that gives her joy and strength to cling to Him. It makes her eager to share God with others that He is real and very kind. Grace's walk with the Lord has been consistent despite many challenges, and she warned, "Anyone who puts his hand to the plough shouldn't look back." She uses this stage of her life to advise and encourage young people to use their strength to do what God has placed in their hands. They should live wisely and when they seek Him, they will find Him. "He says, 'Give me your life and cling to Me, I will help you.' We can do nothing of ourselves, we need to come to Him," Grace said. She attested to God's intervention and help to have kept her alive in spite of the pressures of life. Her continuous prayer is that the Lord would stretch His mighty arm to the people He made and died for to give them eternal life. She affirmed Jesus' words that the harvest is plenty, and we should pray for labourers to be sent into His harvest.

As a senior citizen, well into her senior years, Grace was asked what she would do if she was given another twenty or thirty years to live. She responded, "I would continue His work, asking Him to help me do this. My life is in His hands, and whatever He asks of me, I will do." Her word to Canada is that those in authority should honour God and look to Him to help in the affairs of the nation, affirming His love, and saying, "We will give account of everything we do." She prayed a blessing over the country, that, "The Lord of the universe who made heaven and earth, who feeds all and gives rain, will continue in His love over Canada." Grace also had a word for Israel as a nation. "They are the chosen people of God and He will bring them back to Himself," she said. Grace continued, "My prayer for Israel while surrounding nations make war with them, is that God will rouse Himself on behalf of Israel. He would wake up as a man who slept with wine." She described Israel's position as the true olive tree into which others have been engrafted through Christ.[37] Her prayer is that "God will do it very soon and the whole world will know. When He speaks it will come to pass. He is the God of His Word, the God of time and seasons, no one can stop it." In her usual outburst into songs, Grace began, "The most Excellency is Jesus, shout hallelujah, Amen." Her message to the Body of Christ is that they should pray and that the Lord will help them stand to the end. She prays "they would stick to their confession and the Lord would help them walk in it." And for those who don't have a relationship with Him yet, "that because of His name, His word and His shed blood, God should have mercy on them and help them come to Him and not continue in their own ways." Grace concluded with a message to the world. "My message to the world is to listen to the voice of God," she said, making a reference to Psalm 62:10-12. We opened the Bible and read out the verse. "That's it!" Grace exclaimed. "Power belongs to God only and that God is Jesus Christ," she said, as she began to sing, "The power, the power, the Pentecostal power is just the same today." She continued speaking, "He shall be Lord of all, or not Lord at all. He is Lord and He won't share His glory with anyone. He cannot be bribed. He is the same yesterday, today and forever, to You alone be the glory." The message wasn't complete until mother chorused two songs and we joined her, "To God be the glory, great things He has done…and opened the Lifegate, that all may go in." She sang the other one in Yoruba, her native language, "Enyin lo ye, Baba, Enyin lo ye lati gba ogo." It's translated in English as, "You are worthy, O Lord, You are worthy to receive all the glory!

Mom and children during her granddaughter's wedding in 2014
L - R: Kola, Yemisi, Wole, Eniola, Grace, Kenny, Toyin,
Sope, Ehime, Pelumi

Wole & Eniola's wedding in 2014
L- R: Ehime, Michael, Sope, the groom and bride, Toyin,
Kenny, Tokunbo, Pelumi, Taiwo

Mom's Birthday in 2016. From L to R: Sope, Grace, Yemisi, Taiwo, Gabriel, and his mom, Ehime

Grace with son-in-law, Kola, and daughter, Taiwo at the Rees Street Park, Toronto.

A good pose of Modupe with Grace (2017)

L - R: Judy, Grace, Pam, and Sope
(LoLP team with Grace at first visit)

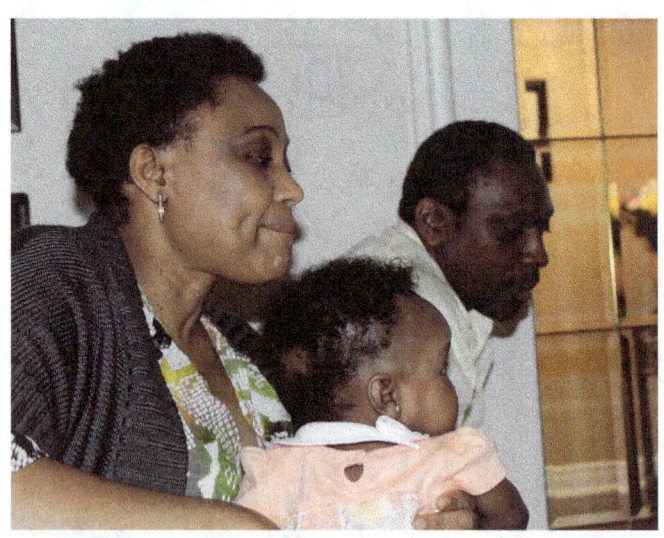

Yemisi with granddaughter Analise, and Pelu during the visit

Grace with daughter, Sope, enjoying the sunshine.

L - R: Taiwo poses with big Sister Yewande and Mom Grace (2019)

David playing "Happy Birthday" at Grandma's 80th birthday party

Grace's well-used Bible

Afterword

It was a wonderful opportunity to hear Grace tell the story of God's amazing grace in her life over the weeks of the interviews. We appreciated our time with her, as she unreservedly answered all the questions asked. It was real and authentic. She gave much content for our work. Just when we felt we were done, we sensed the need to extend the interview to Grace's primary caregivers who are involved in her day-to-day living with their care and support. We thought this would give further testimony. Pam and I scheduled a visit with my sister, Yemisi, and her husband, Kola, whom Grace has lived with since she came to Canada over a decade ago. Their relationship with her as daughter and son-in-law gave deeper insight and greater perspective to Grace's story of God's grace.

Yemisi recalled the early years of growing up with her siblings. Though her mother was strict and wouldn't put up with "nonsense," she was always there for them. She taught the girls how to make a home which later helped them in their journey as wives and mothers.

Yemisi had many memories of family life. Her parents were loving and always celebrated their children. Mom was a seamstress by profession and because of that the children always looked their best especially at church on Sundays. People would look at what they wore and would want their children to have it too. "It was important that we looked our best," Yemisi recalled. Though the family didn't have too much, they managed their resources well as parents raising their children, with special focus on learning and education. She remembered how their mother would cook the meals and also teach the children to do so. Mom would go to the market and as soon as she was home, she would call the children to help in the kitchen. The house would be quiet and even the boys had their chores too. On Friday nights, she would remind them all that Saturday was an early day with lots of cleaning and laundry to be done.

Humorously, Yemisi added that some of the children would try to hide and avoid it, but mom would encourage everyone to get their laundry out. Spiritual training was also a part of their upbringing. A bell kept in Dad's room reminded the children for family prayer every night in the living room. Sharing family fun times together was also important as the family grew up. Yemisi recounted, "We would picnic in the park or on the beach especially on Sunday afternoons and holidays." Their favourite place was Ikoyi Park which was a typical community park on the Lagos Island.

Growing up, the children had different responsibilities in the family. She vividly recalled an incident when her mother gave her some money to go to the store to buy groceries. She lost the money on her way and didn't want to return home. She thought her mother would be angry but was surprised that she was not. That meant quite a lot to her as it encouraged her to be more responsible. The children always had extra help and tutoring with their studies especially in difficult subjects. Their parents' focus, especially mom's, was on spiritual training and character as the kids grew up. Yemisi remarked, "She had a large family and was fortunate that her business was at home. She is a Proverbs 31 woman and juggled so many things." She recalled the time when she was preparing for her entrance exams into secondary school at the age of ten. She remembered her mom's promise that if she did well, she would make her a sailor skirt suit. It was an outfit she had always wanted. She passed her exams well, got three interviews for secondary school, and enrolled in a boarding school outside Lagos. Mom surprised her and made her a sailor suit just as she promised! It was a blue skirt with a white top and had a tie and trims on it. She couldn't have been any happier when she received her present! She added that mom always encouraged them to do well in school.

Mother also had a strategy for resolving conflict among her children. If someone had done something wrong she would bring them all together in the same place. "She wouldn't separate us. She made sure we all got along very well. We knew what she wanted and knew her standards so we tried to keep them. With that we were safe! If we did slip up, other siblings would warn us, and we would definitely be disciplined," Yemisi said.

Growing up in a middle class, conservative and safe neighbourhood, celebrating Christmas was one of the favourite family traditions in the Macarthy family. It was always a big celebration,

Afterword

and everyone looked forward to it. The kids would get new clothes and shoes for both Christmas and New Year. Going to the city to visit Father Christmas whose grotto was powered by an in-door train ride for kids, was a special highlight of the festive season. Everyone received gifts from Santa, and at home there was always lots to eat and drink. The family shared special Christmas dishes with both their Christian and non-Christian neighbours, which the children would take to them, and the neighbours would give coins to appreciate the child who brought the goodies! Reminiscing, Yemisi said, "We all wanted to go to a particular neighbour who was very generous!"

The kids in the neighbourhood knew each other and played creatively together. Though mom was encouraging and supportive of her children's friendships and relationships, she remained very cautious. Most Saturday mornings were cleaning days, and for catching up on homework. Yemisi remembered a friend coming to the house to invite her out on a Saturday morning. Mom asked after the girl's parents and asked her why she wasn't at home helping out. She told the girl to go back home and help out her mother. That girl never came back. At that time, Yemisi was embarrassed, but she soon came to understand the reason for her mom's action as she grew up.

Mom was always the stricter parent. The children at times tried to get around dad, but he would look away, and always stuck with mom's judgment. Yemisi spoke of their parents' marriage. "They definitely had their challenges as a couple, but they had a good marriage. They understood each other, and they worked together," she said. She spoke of some of her mom's qualities. "She was always very consistent. She was very upfront and very caring and still is today. She is selfless, and these attributes are still there, and the children can see it too." She spoke further, "She hits the nail on the head and is not afraid to speak up. She had her moods, but we would back off and try to manage it as best we can. Right now as she is older, we accommodate more." Yemisi mentioned that the children were influenced by those qualities their mother raised them with. Good character, faith, love for family and home, and integrity were a big part of the process. "We create a balance now and learn from both the present and from our new environment.

We depend on God's wisdom to work through our lives today, to know what works while still gleaning from the past," she revealed.

The family had times of difficulties and challenges. She remembered some of those times and how her parents went through them. She recalled being in the third year of secondary school when the first son and brother passed away from sickle cell disease. "That really shook our foundations as a family, especially mom," she said. She remembered how difficult it was, going home on holiday the first time after the incident. However over time, God used everything to bring about their salvation. It was hard for mom to get to that point as she was really affected by the loss. However, with time God carried her through, and it became the point for a personal relationship with Jesus. Her husband and children followed, and from that moment, she didn't look back.

Yemisi further added, "Lots of people initially criticized mom's drastic change in her new found love for the Lord, but she didn't let their remarks or actions deter her from her decision." After the incident, the other children had to go through medical tests to see if any had the disease and it was an extremely traumatic experience as two others were then diagnosed with it. The family thought they would be going through the same experience as with their oldest brother again, but God's grace was sufficient.

Yemisi studied in Nigeria up to her university years. She went through the difficult times with mother, as the older sister, Toyin, had travelled to England to continue her studies. She recalled their mother got a Word from God which she shared with her when she was much younger. Her mother's faith grew, and God promised He would not allow anything to repeat the past – God took control. "My siblings still had the disease, but God took control, and just as He promised my mother, His power and sufficiency were enough as they continued to live with it. Sometimes they would get sick as a result, and they would have to be hospitalized, but God was with them day after day, year after year," Yemisi recounted.

Mom and Dad always had their ways to encourage their children's dreams and goals as they grew up. Yemisi shared, "We all had dreams and she encouraged us with the big steps. We always felt celebrated and supported." If the children gained admission into high school or post-secondary school, her mother always recognized it as a special achievement. Her father always encouraged them to do their best and to follow their dreams. "He would help with tutoring which was costly then, and mom would chip in. Dad would always say, "Not to worry, you will get there, even if it is not happening now, it will happen, just persevere and focus," she recalled.

Their parents were part of their lives and were always there cheering their kids. "We followed our dreams and were always supported financially, emotionally, with prayer, and with provisions that we needed," Yemisi smiled. When she got admission to study Law at University, it was tough, but they encouraged her. "When you shared what God was doing in your life with them, they always encouraged you," she concluded.

Yemisi first met her husband, Kola, during her second year of university. "I had a summer job at a bank in the city where Kola happened to be working. He studied in America and was back in Nigeria to work," she narrated. She spoke about her mom's influence, with respect to her advice and input regarding her future husband. "She didn't control anyone, but we knew she was praying, and she wasn't afraid to speak to anyone when she needed to." Yemisi at that time was religious but was not "born again." Mom always invited and welcomed their friends in the home. Occasionally, she would chip in some questions, and say their lives would be much better with Jesus. Kola was also a nominal Christian when he was introduced to the family. He found the family very welcoming, especially his mother-in-law. "She was very open minded and embraced me," Kola said. He added, "She made me feel comfortable, appreciated and always gave me the best food in the house!" He described his mother-in-law as very accommodating. He was initially puzzled by the "Christian thing" she often talked about. "Everything revolved around being born again. You would have a general discussion and it would get back to the salvation message," he said.

After some time, he realized it was important to her and he wasn't offended by it. She didn't impose it in any way but naturally and wisely, brought it into discussions. She didn't put any pressure. "She was so beyond the now that she didn't judge, but continuously encouraged and this helped us in our Christian journey," Kola said. She made it easy to fit into the family unlike his father-in-law who was quite upfront and would ask him a lot of questions about his background, his intentions and plans. Kola added jokingly of his father-in-law, "He would ask me, 'Hey, what do you want?'" When he met the family, his own father had passed away and his father-in-law became a father figure to him. He learned from him. It helped him to speak up and play the expected role and responsibility of the man in the African context. A role that he now fits into as a father-in-law himself.

Even after Kola and Yemisi got married, they continued to have close contact with her parents. Their new home as a young couple was only twenty minutes away. Mom and Taiwo were always coming to help when they had little ones. After about a month, mom would return, but Taiwo sometimes stayed longer. Even when Yemisi and her family moved to a farther residence forty minutes away from her parents, they would visit. After some time, it happened that Taiwo didn't have to return to the family home in Falolu as she was so used to Yemisi from childhood. Taiwo now lived with Yemisi. God was behind the scenes orchestrating the process for the fulfilment of His purpose and plan for the entire family.

Kola and Yemisi came to Christ after getting married. They had attended church but were not "born –again" or "Spirit-filled," as they said. Yemisi came to know Christ personally through a colleague at the Lagos State Ministry of Justice, where they both worked as state counsels. She shared with Yemisi about receiving the infilling of the Holy Spirit and not long after, invited her home for prayer fellowship. Kola was going to drive her there, but he wouldn't be staying. Yemisi's colleague and her husband both opened the Scriptures to her. They placed their hands on her and prayed and she was filled with the Holy Spirit. When she got back home, she spoke in tongues, and Kola noticed right away that she was excited about God. She immediately decided to change churches from the Anglican Church they attended to Christ Chapel, a Pentecostal church. Kola also followed, and soon he was filled with the Holy Spirit.

They are both sure that Grace's prayers had much to do with it. Kola was brought up in a Christian home that was Anglican based, but meeting with Yemisi's mom from a Pentecostal setting, made him realise there was quite a difference. "It was from private and liturgical to external and exuberant," he remarked. He finally began to understand what his mother-in-law had been saying all along about love and grace. What they had seen in mom prepared them for this great change in their lives.

The plans for Kola and Yemisi to emigrate to Canada began to surface. Kola's brother, Lakunle Fashogbon, who lives in America told him to look into the immigration initiative in Canada. He began praying about it, but Yemisi did not welcome the idea initially. After some months of praying, God opened her heart up to the proposal, and the process began fully. Looking back now, they see it was God who planned it all. His hand was in the whole process because a lot of things smoothly fell into place. God had the bigger picture. Today, Kola and Yemisi are the primary caregivers for her mom and sister, part of the journey that started long before the thoughts of coming to Canada.

Yemisi and her husband's application forms for immigration did not encourage them to include Taiwo because of her developmental disability; a clause that could have denied their application. They moved to Canada with their children, but still wanted to bring Taiwo. Yemisi was always thinking of Taiwo's future, especially with their parents getting older.

After two years, Kola and Yemisi invited the family to visit. So in 2001, they applied for visiting visas from the Canadian Embassy in Nigeria. Each applicant had to appear for an interview. But their application landed on the desk of a lady they knew. She was the wife of someone whom Kola and Yemisi had worked with in Christian missions. The application was processed without Taiwo going for an interview, opening an opportunity to visit Canada. "Once they were back in Nigeria, we wanted them to return here," Yemisi narrated. She further narrated, She continued, "We discussed with my Dad about keeping Taiwo with us, and the only way that could work was if they re-applied to come again." It was considered that she and Kola could sponsor her parents and Taiwo under their care.

However, her mom wasn't really planning a permanent stay in Canada and dad was not happy with the extreme cold weather. "He was not interested, but we said once Taiwo's application was processed here, then Mom and Dad could go back to Nigeria," Yemisi added.

Afterword

They applied for visiting visas again, and for the second time, the same thing happened! Taiwo and her parents didn't have to show up at the Embassy! About that time, God showed Yemisi a dream. There was a person called Andrew, who had lived with the Macarthy family in Nigeria when the children were growing up. They called him "brother" as it was through the church he came to live with them. She saw Andrew in the dream. He was at the door and rang the bell and had brought Taiwo to them. He then left after he handed Taiwo to them at the door. She believed it was an angel in the dream who did that. That dream gave them hope to keep going, although it was a very difficult process. They started to file their papers and commenced with the immigration protocols. As soon as they knew Taiwo had a disability, the problems started. And while they were making progress with sponsorship application in Canada, Dad passed away. The family went through a mourning period, and the visiting visas got close to expiry. "They had to make a decision to either stay in Nigeria or come to Canada. Mom prayed and decided to bring Taiwo to Canada during that time," Yemisi recounted. She further narrated,

"Unfortunately, there was a strike in Nigeria at the time. The labour union shut down everything. No one could enter or leave the country. They now had a short time left on their visa. They had booked a flight, and a few days before they were due to leave, the strike was called off! Taiwo was on her way! It was such a great testimony! That's how they came here. Mom was willing to sacrifice her mourning period and leave her home to come and stay for Taiwo. Now, my husband and I could apply for humanitarian and compassionate consideration as Dad had passed away, and Mom was left with a disabled child. Through it all God was weaving everything together. There was still a possibility of being denied, and a psychologist's assessment was necessary for Taiwo. The first question he asked us was, "Is this person here in this country?" We answered, "Yes," and he added, "fight on for her," Yemisi recalled. "God indeed does take care, and He sees the total picture. We are limited but He is unlimited," she said.

With a growing family and having full-time businesses, as well as church and community involvements, Kola and Yemisi both shared how they cope with caring for Mom and Taiwo.

Yemisi spoke, "We both depend on God's grace. For anything He orders, He gives sufficient grace. It becomes possible because the grace is there." She continued, "It has never looked like it is impossible. Sometimes it is overwhelming, but He supplies the grace and encourages you and gives you the push." "Everything in the home is a learning process," Kola began. He spoke further, "The kids are learning from what we are doing and how God is helping. It will come to their time because they know all about it. They have been part of the caregiving and they understand." He mentioned that their Grandma is a prayer warrior and she prays for everything. She is also an encourager, and she encourages them in their endeavours. When needed, she scolds them, and they learn from her life in the way she relates with their parents and their actions with her. He explained that this is preparing them also for their future and the responsibilities God has for them. Certainly, there are challenges, physical, emotional, health, financial and others in caring for an elderly person.

Kola described how his family manages these. "The biggest challenge would have been health," he said. "That would be the biggest fear, but God has been good and given them good health." Taiwo and mom have both been living with them for over thirteen years now with no major sickness. "There was a fall requiring medical help for mom, but apart from that, her health has been good for her age." Kola revealed. With a sense of humour, he remarked, "Taiwo is going to last forever! She likes only certain foods such as bread, egg, sardine, and tea among others! It's a wonderful thing to see what God can do." He recalled sharing with someone who was very discouraged with his difficulties. Kola encouraged him with his own story of God's faithfulness even in the challenges. He used his mother-in-law as a point of reference of his testimony to his visitor. "My mother-in-law here, is a great source of blessing. Her presence has given us a lot of encouragement," he remarked. He drew a parallel from the life of Obededom in the Bible whom God had blessed because he received the ark of covenant into his house.

Kola revealed that God had prepared them ahead for the task as both his grandmothers before their passing, lived with him and Yemisi at different times in Nigeria. So they were used to care giving. "We are obedient and give glory to God; He has always provided," he said. He continued, "We all have a part in God's purpose, even Taiwo has a purpose." Yemisi described her mother's strengths and weaknesses at this stage of life. With a growing family now, and as grandparents themselves, they still find the time and balance to give care and assistance to mom and Taiwo in their daily living. "Taiwo usually helps mom when she needs something, and she is a great companion to mom," Yemisi said. Humorously she added, "But when baby Analise (Kola and Yemisi's first grandchild) arrived, Taiwo abandoned mom for Anna!"

She revealed that there have been some noticeable changes in mom's mood due to age. "She has some arthritis pains and has to use a walker to assist her movement. This is difficult for someone who has always been on the move," Yemisi mentioned. She spoke of the grace of God as the anchor that keeps her mom going. "She embraces His grace, and she still has some independence to an extent. It's sometimes hard to get around as you age and of course the stairs make it even more difficult since her fall. She was able to walk around the block in the neighbourhood before, but this is curtailed, now. However, mom is constantly encouraged to go to church for the senior's ministry and she often helps prepare meals. The most important project for mom is her prayer ministry and encouraging everyone around her. She has also developed a new love for gardening and still loves to watch wrestling on television in her room. "Kola takes her for outings and she has so much fun she doesn't ever want to return home! She enjoyed some time with us in New York, recently, and had a trip to Niagara Falls." Yemisi spoke extensively of her mom.

For Kola, his mother-in-law's greatest sphere of influence is her faith in God. He spoke, "Everything about her revolves around Jesus and her faith in Him. She continually lives it out in her everyday life, and there's evidence of a two-way relationship. She is such an encouragement to each of us in our relationship with God. Her prayer life is remarkable, and it has changed the lives of her children."

Kola is a leader in the Prayer ministry at the Pickering Pentecostal Church since coming to Canada. He was brought up in a home where they were always encouraged to pray. He also married into a family that prays consistently. "When you put it together, it is a big thing in your life," he commented. They try to model that to their children also. They can see the importance of a prayer life. Kola described the legacy his mother-in-law has passed to the next generation. He concluded, "She has given an example of contentment in life. She is a hard worker with a strong sense of duty. She was a housewife, a business woman and contractor in Lagos. She is an encourager. She reminds me of Proverbs 31, and the whole family rise up and call her "blessed!""

Reward

Reward her for all she has done. Let her deeds publicly declare her praise.
(Proverbs 31:31) NLT

She is my mother. I have always known her since she gave birth to me. She is a godly mother and brought her children up in the fear of God. She provided for her family and cared for us all; a virtuous woman she is indeed. The words that best describe my mother are: A woman of Integrity – She stands by what she says; a woman of Prayer – She is consistent in her prayer life and committed to praying for everyone; and a woman that gave her all – She is humble and has served all the people the Lord brought her way.

When I was leaving my family in Nigeria for England at the age of twenty-one, I remembered my mother had really encouraged me and paid my fees to help me further my education and reminded me that I am not alone in my journey, that the Lord is with me. This helped me all the way. Words cannot describe this woman of God, only God can reward her labour of love for her family, the Body of Christ and even her grandchildren. God bless you, Mama.

- ***Oloruntoyin A. Ogunsan***

She is my mother. My mum has always been God-fearing, but I will say my mum has changed in many ways since about 1973 when she became a believer after the loss of her first son, my elder brother. The words that best describe her person to me are: Committed: To God and to loved ones. She would sacrifice her time and resources to bring smiles. Compassionate: No one comes to mum and leaves the same; she will pray and meet physical needs if necessary. Consistent: I believe because she has enjoyed God's mercy and grace, she is consistent in administering the love of God.

I vividly remembered the sacrifice my mother made for me to finish my Advanced Level education in Abeokuta, in Ogun State in Nigeria. I was very ill, almost at the point of death. As there were no rooms for family to stay in the hospital, she slept underneath a tree day and night outside the hospital until I was discharged. Later, she travelled with me to the exam centre almost daily to write my exams, a distance of over 100 miles on dangerous roads.

- ***Victor Kenny Macarthy***

I am her son-in-law. I met her sometime in 1982. When I first met my mother-in-law, I perceived her as a "serious character". In the first instance, she would tolerate no messing about when tasks needed to be completed. She is, however, kind, very caring and wise with plenty of knowledge; dependable and sympathetic. These qualities I believe have not changed greatly, just gotten a bit more relaxed, I would say. The words that best describe her to me are: Availability: A tendency to make her own schedule or priorities secondary to those wishing counsel; Compassionate – As she will seek to help heal the hurts of others; Contentment – The knowledge and understanding that true happiness does not depend on material things but the Almighty God alone.

I have had opportunities to enjoy her cooking and found my stay at the family house in Falolu most enjoyable every time.

My mother-in-law has also opened her home on many occasions for night prayers to be conducted which has impacted many people's lives and mine. My prayer and hope is that she will continue to be blessed abundantly, and continue to have good health as well as live even longer, amen.

- Adetokunbo A. Ogunsan

Mummy Grace Macarthy is my mother. I am her last born. My impression of her is that she is a true woman of God and passionately loves God and the things of God. She hasn't changed over time. She has stood the test of time and that has made her closer to God even at her age. The three words that best describes her are: Loving, Giver and Selfless.

She loves people not only in words but also in deed. You can tell she's genuine in actions and she meant good to everyone that comes her way. She doesn't hold back in terms of giving financially, materially and spiritually. She's a true giver. She has given her time in praying, fasting and ministering of the Word without collecting from individuals and ministries. She has proven her selflessness in the past and present. She has been there for individuals that needed her help in the community and ministry. Her service and dedication to the work of God is exceptional. I remember years ago when I was going through a lot in my life, I had serious challenges. God used her to pray, encourage and support me through those times. There was miracle and testimony that resulted from those challenges. I thank God for sustaining her life.

-Pelumi Macarthy

I am a son-in-law of Grace Olaide Macarthy but I call her 'mom'. I consider her as my biological mother. I did not know what to expect before I met her almost 30 years ago. But since I set my eyes on her, she has treated me like anyone would their own child whom they love, and this relationship has been so ever since. To find three words only to describe Mummy Macarthy is a bit difficult. It is like being asked to pick out three outstanding stars on a star studded summer night. This being said, I will start by saying what readily comes to you as you engage Mummy is her Love for the Lord Jesus. Her love of Christ, has seen her being born of a royal background yet casting all aside to inherit the eternal kingdom of our blessed Savior, Jesus Christ. My late mother testified that Mummy was always evangelizing in the local markets and that was how she came to know her.

Secondly, her strength of character - very few people would reject the temptations of laying their hands-on millions of dollars and pounds sterling, particularly if offered with no strings attached. On two different occasions, such huge monies were brought to her as loot stars stars on a star studded summer night. This being said, I will start by saying what readily comes to you as you engage Mummy is her Love for the Lord Jesus. Her love of Christ, has seen her walk away from worldly wealth and accolades, them all away. Finally, her forthrightness. Mom is a no-nonsense individual. No matter on whose side you are, if you are not standing in the path of truth, you are likely to be offended by her. Severally when family decisions are being made and Mummy is consulted, she will point the entire family to what the Lord put in her heart by the Holy Bible.

Her kindness is truly legendary. While preparing for my marriage to my wife, Mummy called me one evening when I came visiting and wanted to know the state of my preparations. I told her everything was under control and had been sorted out. Then she asked me specifically if I have picked up my suit, and I replied with some righteous excuse. Then she proceeded to inquire how much was left. I told her not to worry about it, but she insisted and that was how the balance was paid.

-Michael Chiadika

Mummy Grace Macarthy is my aunt. I was adopted by Mama and late Papa Macarthy when my mother, late Mrs. Esther Bada, passed away in 1977. She and my mother are sisters. That said, I do not see Mama as my aunt, but as my mother. My relationship with Mummy began right from when I was born. I was told I always wanted to be with her prior to my mum's passing. I was brought up by her, and absolutely take after her both in mannerism and looks. Mummy Macarthy is one of a kind. Very straightforward, caring, loving and God fearing. This has not changed over time; she is ever so fervent in theLord which has now passed on to us her children, grandchildren and great-grandchildren.

I am close to Mummy and often phone her in Canada when I miss that motherly love and attention which I'm used to. The three words that best describe her to me are: Caring – I had always suffered from dysmenorrhea, and when that time of the month would come, I remember mummy with menthol, balm and hot water bottle sitting with me and praying over me. My mum is caring but firm and passionate (in her walk with the Lord). Looking back now, I value the days when she would take us to the Gospel Centre church. I am so very grateful for her. My walk with the Lord is as a result of her fervency. Faith – My mum is a woman of great faith! Praise God! My life is a testimony because of her and how she has brought me up.

There are many memories and wonderful stories but not enough pages to write them all. The most significant event in my life was when I gave my life to Christ. Mummy was present with me and stood by me praying over me in Yoruba dialect. It was a special day indeed, one I won't forget. I also remember

when I was younger, due to my love for all things sugary, I had tooth decay such that my teeth were brown, and the dentist advised that every tooth be removed. Mummy said no and prayed over me and oneby one, the Lord gave me a new set of teeth! I love her so much.
- ***Modupe Mann***

My Grandma is a strong-hearted woman that can impart knowledge and wisdom in any situation. My favorite attribute about her is her experiences from life, as she uses it to help others in various situations in their own lives. There are many fond memories of her. My grandma never ceases to uplift me and put a smile on my face. She has influenced me through her wisdom and experiences in life, of how to overcome situations and circumstances, and this helps me to keep a positive attitude at all times. I have learnt to stay strong in faith and rely on Jesus Christ in any situation.
- ***Seun Ogunsan***

My Grandma is a fervent praying woman, with a big heart and unquestionable love for God. Her humour is captivating, she has a sweet side and an iron hand. She is straight talking; does not mince her words for anybody – I love that! It's scary sometimes.

One of my fond memories of grandma was when she visited London in 2015. While staying at my house, I decided one day on my way back from work, to get her the British "delicacy" of fish and chips. To my surprise, grandma was excited and told me she had been looking forward to eating this since she came from Canada. She really appreciated that I had her in mind. Her reaction taught me that it's the small things that count, and this will always have an impact on me!

She has taught me to trust God despite what circumstances may look like. The stories she tells of her life are a testament in trusting in and putting Him first. Her spiritual legacy will always encourage me to fight the good fight of faith in Christ Jesus!

- Moriayo Ogunsan

Grandma hasn't seemed to age in about 20 years! Gentle but powerful, disciplined and strict but loving and joyful. She is very fair, and she always seems to know what's going on in your life before you even do, she is very discerning.

My fondest memory was when I was a kid and she was in London visiting, it was after a Sunday service and I really wanted to go off and play with some kids from the church at their house. She didn't want me to go and was calling my name to come back but I ignored her and carried on about my business... I thought she's grandma, she's a softy... oh how wrong was I! When I got home, she called me and told me what I did was wrong then proceeded to give me a good spanking, I tried to dodge but that's when I realized how nimble she was!

She has influenced me in a positive way always encouraging me motivating me to be a better person and to put God first in all I do that is something I will never forget about her, God first... everything else will follow that is the legacy she has left for me.

- *Femi Ogunsan*

My Grandma is passionate, loving, kind, stoic, respected, a matriarch, leader, and role model. She is an amazing woman of

God. My favourite attribute about her is her leadership style. It amazes me how gentle and calm she always remains. She may go for hours in a room full of people and not say a word, but as soon as she speaks, all eyes are on her, and everyone listens. Most fond memories I can recall of my grandma have been set in her bedroom. She always has a word of wisdom and a prayer for you when you visit her. I remember on her 80th birthday in that same room, I cameon her 80th birthday in that same room, I came over in a tuxedo and played "Happy Birthday" on the saxophone for her. She has influenced me in many ways. She models how to lead, how to listen, and how to always be a blessing. I think her biggest way of influencing me is her influence on my mother. I believe my grandmother has had probably the biggest impact on helping my mother become the woman she is today. I believe a legacy is made not by what you have or can do, but by the lives you've affected. I know my grandmother has impacted so many lives in so many different positive ways.

- ***JesusFunnaya David Chiadika***

My Grandma is a beautiful and an amazing woman of God. She often has few words, but those words mean much when she speaks. She is kind, strong, witty, compassionate, passionate, and is the most 'spiritual' person I know. It is a running joke in the family that Grandma can see "through you" when she looks at you. She has a formidable strength about her, and an ability to live in wisdom - qualities I see in my Mom, and that I hope to carry and imbibe also. Grandma's life and faith in Christ is an inspiration to me, and it is amazing to see and hear about the miracles God does and is doing in her life. Her legacy is like a flame ever-burning; bringing light and life to all those who encounter it.

- *JesusMiracle Chiadika*

My Grandma is very compassionate, strong, funny, and has so much faith in God. I love the way she cares about others, even if it's a stranger she's never met before. My favourite thing about her are her grey eyes, because you know exactly what she's saying when she just looks at you. One of my fond memories I can recall is when she taught me how to sew. After that, I felt like a fashionista! Though I only learned the basics, it encouraged my sense of creativity and ingenuity. I love my Grandma so much and she has taught me that it is highly important to have a strong relationship with God.

- JesusNewness Chiadika

Grandma Macarthy (aka "my neighbour" as we call each other) is the most significant spiritual influence in my life. She is loving, caring, compassionate and empathic. She is the embodiment of the type of spirituality that challenges everyone around her. I can testify of her bold and fearless approach to life and how it has positively affected her family, friends and even strangers. My favourite attribute about her is her strength in many areas. One of the fondest memories of Grandma Macarthy is a specific story that she reminds me of from time to time about my childhood and how it changed how she saw me as a person. That story has stuck with me as it has guided my outlook on my spirituality.

She has influenced me spiritually and emotionally through the many prayers and bible verses we have covered over the years. She has been there for me whenever I needed to talk about anything that might not be going as planned. Her advice has helped me get over several hurdles that the enemy placed before me, and her prayers have helped me break the shackles that sin had on me. She has passed on to me a spiritual legacy that I have witnessed first-hand and will pass on to my children. The lessons I have learned from her over the years will probably require a novel of my own.

- Oluwatoni Abrahams

Grandma is a God-fearing woman and very devoted spiritually. She is loving and kind and goes out of her way to help others. She helped me through my high school years. When I would have problems, I would go straight to her room, and we would talk about what happened and ways I could fix the problem. She would also pray for me daily. Grandma has influenced me to be a more selfless person and look out for others before myself. I have received a spiritual legacy from her. Grandma has taught me that our faith in Jesus Christ is very important and that it is very important to get close to God because He is the only one who can help you in your times of need. She will not always be there to help us go through some troubles.

- Jesurotimi Abrahams

My grandma is very prayerful, selfless, spiritual and funny with an introverted personality. She loves her family and has a genuine love for people. My favourite attribute about my grandma is her wittiness. Very few people get to see this side of my grandma, but she has some hilarious one liners and is very quick on her feet when it comes to comebacks. When I had my bunion surgery, I was up all-night crying in pain after the anaesthesia had worn off. My grandma stayed up all night beside my bed praying for me and comforting me. She didn't go to bed until I fell asleep. She has shown me that you are never alone in your deepest valleys when you have a relationship with Jesus. The effectual fervency of prayer is definitely the most important legacy my grandma has given me. No amount of wealth could ever compare with that.

- ***Dami Abrahams***

Grandma is one of a kind. She is very sweet and loving, yet bold and truthful when it relates with her Faith is God.

Grandma is an encourager. This is just one of the many gifts of the Spirit she clearly possesses and exhibits. Many many times, I have witnessed how she uses the truth of the bible with prayers and her love for people to lift up their spirits, and I am also a testament to that fact.

If I haven't mentioned it yet, my Grandma LOVES people. She loves her family; her children and their spouses, grandchildren and their spouses and great-grandchildren. And she loves to make sure all our stomachs are satisfied! Grandma, when she had the physical strength, loved to cook! I remember growing up, on so many Sundays, when we visit, I looked forward to the great meals she would prepare. I have even learned some of her cooking recipes that I enjoy using today.

Grandma has influenced me in so many ways. She is a great role model for me as a wife, mother, daughter, friend and follower of Jesus Christ. When faced with any issue, I can look back and recall how I've seen or heard my grandma respond to similar issues and/or what she will say and do in similar situations.

One thing I have learned from grandma is to put God first in EVERYTHING I do. She would always say that even if she may not have all the material things to give that could meet my physical or emotional needs, she is leaving me with the knowledge of the greatest gift that she or anyone can give me; which is the truth of the word of God. She has taught me to keep to the path of Christ and to make sure I pass the same legacy to the next generation coming. I have also learned from my grandma the importance of being a prayerful Christian.

- Eniola Daramola

Grandma Macarthy is "down to earth" and very genuine. She treats people equally regardless of your relationship to her and on a spiritual level, is the perfect example of what a Christian should be. She is bold and unafraid to speak her heart which I admire her for. My favorite attribute about her is her valiance. I wouldn't say I have one specific memory, rather, an ongoing one. This is in the way she values her Christianity above money, property and even other people. Grandma has influenced me in the type of person I've become and maybe my dress sense too. I have received a legacy of the importance of the Bible, prayer and Christian values from her.

- *Jonathan Macarthy*

Grandma Macarthy is a strong vibrant woman who I respect ever so much and look up to. My favorite attribute about her is her ability to speak the truth. I admire the courage she shows to speak up in situations where others can't. One of my fond memories of Grandma and its impact on me was when I accidentally set fire to my parents' kitchen and I obviously as you can imagine was terribly scared and fearful. My grandma showed so much bravery there was not an ounce of fear in her eyes. Despite the challenging pain she had on her leg, she was able to stand and wait for the Fire brigade to assist us. I will forever respect and cherish her. She didn't judge me in this situation, rather she made me laugh to take my mind off the fact that I almost burned the whole house down. She has influenced me to trust God and always put Jesus first in all that I do.

- Joanna Macarthy

Good
Radiant
Amazing
Nice
Disciplined
Modest
Amiable

- Gabriel and Gideon Macarthy

She is my in-law – my daughter is married to her son. We met in 1992 when she came with her husband to ask for our daughter's hand in marriage. She was precise and took care to be accurate and exact about the time the Holy Spirit ministered to her in a particular way that led her to conclude that she was asking for the right person to marry her son. This perception has not changed a bit. The words that best describe her in our relationship so far are: Prayerful - Mama is noted for her consistent prayer life; Passionate - She has strong feelings of enthusiasm for reaching out with the Gospel. She's always interested in sharing the Good News of the love of God to all. Commitment – Her commitment to the things of the Kingdom are unparalleled.

I recall going to thank Mama for something she did for me. She immediately objected and said, "My sister, give all thanks to Jesus." Since then I have learnt to thank Jesus for whatever is done for me by anyone and equally tell people to thank Him if I do anything for others. Mama is thorough, and highly disciplined. She hates to sit down with people who are discussing the affairs of this world. She would rather pick her Bible and be studying. Her identity in Christ alone keeps her going. Mama lives a productive life of caring, loving, and encouraging all the people around her. Her consistent Christian living is an inspiration to me. I see that nothing in this world can separate mama from doing the work of God. She is a woman of few words, but she feels more comfortable with people who want to sing praises to God, who want to pray, who want to share the love of God. A great evangelist who will abandon her car, if it fails to work within five minutes of starting the engine and thereafter trek kilometers to go to the church for her meetings. She builds a family of Christ, not in-laws.

- Mrs. Florence Akinwale

She is a mother-figure to us. We met her in the early 90's. She is someone who has a deep fellowship with God, a woman of extraordinary faith. The words that best describe her arePrayerful, Heaven-oriented and full of Godly counsel. She has had the grace to bring all her children to Christ.

- Rev. Wale & Bola Grillo,
Christ Harvest Centre

She is a mother to me. She is a pastor of pastors. I met her first at the Gospel Centre Church, now called Winners Gospel Centre. She is a Spirit-filled woman with godly character. She has constantly remained rooted and steadfast in the Lord from the time I met her till the time she travelled out of Nigeria. The
words that best describe to me are: Godly: She is an expression of the fruit of the Spirit: loving, patient, slow to anger and self-disciplined; Committed – though she lived far from church, she would always attend service punctually and regularly (both weekly and Sunday services). Giver: She gives of her substance to the Lord's work. She never keeps her money away from church projects.

I remember when I had an argument with my wife over a place my wife wanted me to go, then I had no car. Mummy intervened and released her driver and car to take me and my wife to the place. She is very kind, nice and very hospitable.

-Joshua Oluwatobi Martins
Pastor, Winners Gospel Centre Lagos, Nigeria

Expressions of GRACE

What is GRACE?
Gained **R**ighteousness **A**t **C**hrist's **E**xpense

Christ purchased for us a right relationship with God that we couldn't earn ourselves because:
Grace is **R**eceived **A**nd **C**an't be **E**arned.

And once this **G**ift is **R**ealized, it **A**dequately **C**overs **E**verything

Every debt is cancelled. Every single sin: past- present –future

So, **G**et **R**eady **A**nd **C**ome **E**xpectantly

Because, **G**race is a **G**rowing **R**evolution **A**nd **C**arnal **E**xecution

Meaning leaving the flesh behind, dying more and more to ourselves and stepping into a movement that continues to change the world by:

Giving **R**edemption **A**nd **C**ommunion to **E**veryone.

God is: **G**ranting **R**est **A**fter **C**ondemnation **E**nds

Because a: **G**ap has been **R**ealized **A**nd **C**onnected **E**ntirely

A Bridge has been built, The Battle has been won: **G**od **R**eigns **A**nd **C**hrist is **E**xalted

GRACE is proof that: **G**od **R**eally **A**lways **C**an **E**ndure

-Excerpt from: The Anima Series (Spoken Word) by Jon Jorgenson

About the Author

Mosope Macarthy-Chiadika has a passion and call of God to write. Her first book, *Jewel of God*, also a biography was published in England in 2007 where she lived before moving to Canada. Mosope lives in Ontario with her family. When she's not writing, Mosope loves to spend time with family and friends. She enjoys reading, travelling, gardening and extends her creativity to home decorating.

Endnotes

1. 1828 Webster's Dictionary, p2
2. Excerpt from "The Grace of God" by Andy Stanley copyright Andy Stanley Published by Thomas Nelson, p3
3. Luke 18: 18-23, p17
4. Olori- traditional name given to the king's wife, the queen, p19
5. Colossians 1:13, p27
6. 2 Kings 6: 16, p29
7. John 21: 25, p38
8. Judges 6:11-14, p39
9. Zechariah 4:6, p39
10. John 14: 11, p47
11. 1 Corinthians 15: 19, p50
12. Hebrews 5:4 , p55
13. Ephesians 2:10, p59
14. Luke 5:5, p61
15. Luke 22:32, p61
16. Mark 2: 21 & 22, p64
17. Luke 15: 11-27, p67
18. Psalm 8:4, p69
19. Luke 24:13-34, p70
20. Henry Francis Lyte – Author of Abide with me (1847), p70
21. 1 Corinthians 12:4-6, p71
22. 1 Corinthians 12:8, p72
23. Ezekiel 37:1-3, p72

24. 1 Corinthians 12:9, p73
25. Isaiah 45:11, p73
26. Mark 4: 35-41, p88
27. Lyrics by Francis J Crosby (1869)https://library.timelesstruths.org/music/Near_the_Cross/, p88
28. Hebrews 12:2, p89
29. Acts 9:3-5, p92
30. 2 Kings 5:14 &17, p92
31. Matthew 8:2-3, p93
32. Psalm 71:18, p94
33. John 17:20, p95
34. John 15:5, p95
35. 1 Kings 8: 21 & 22 p, 95
36. John 14: 16-17, p95
37. Romans 11:17, p99

www.ingramcontent.com/pod-product-compliance
Lightning Source LLC
Chambersburg PA
CBHW071452080526
44587CB00014B/2075